All the World

A Trilogy of One-Acts by Erin Dealey

Uproar Theatrics

LICENSING & PRODUCTION INQUIRIES
Uproar Theatrics, LLC.
hello@uproartheatrics.com I www.UproarTheatrics.com

All the World, A Trilogy of One-Acts by Erin Dealey
Brillig copyright © 2023 by Erin Dealey
What Light? copyright © 2023 by Erin Dealey
Yes, And… copyright © 2024 by Erin Dealey

All the World is published by Uproar Theatrics, LLC
500 8th Ave FRNT 3, #1714 New York, NY 10018

ISBN: 978-1-968051-05-1

First Printing, April 2025

Table of Contents

Brillig 1

What Light? 48

Yes, And... 92

Brillig

<u>Cast of Characters</u>

ALEX: F or M, freshman, haunted by the need to be perfect.

SADIE: F, freshman, haunted by things unsaid. Sadie finds the social-emotional support group useless. It's her last time attending.

STELLA:F, freshman, communicates through haikus and hauntingly odd ukulele tunes.

HILLARY: F or M, subbing for Dr. Randall as facilitator of the social-emotional support group. Does not believe in ghosts.

GHOST OF HAMLET'S FATHER : M, think Darth Vader meets Sir Lawrence Olivier, playing the ghost of the actor who played the ghost in Hamlet long ago (You read that correctly).

GERTRUDE : F or M, ghost of the actor who played Hamlet's mother, with the essence of Moira Rose meets Auntie Mame.

OPHELIA: F or M, ghost of the actor who played Ophelia. Essence of Alexis Rose or David Rose – you decide – meets Emily Webb.

LOCKSMITH: M, offstage voice, afraid of anything that goes bump in the night. Can be double cast with the actor who plays the ghost of the actor who played the Ghost of Hamlet's Father.

What Light?

<u>Cast of Characters</u>

NURSE: F. 1 part Mary Poppins + 2 parts Lorelai Gilmore

JAKE: M. 20ish college sophomore, fresh from an unexpected break-up

LUCY: F. 18ish, freshman, theater major, with a possible break that may ruin her big break

FINN: F. 18ish, Don't-call-me-Elizabeth freshman, suspected of breaking-and-entering.

R.A.: F. 22ish grad student, Pre-law/ Sociology, hoping for a break-through with FINN.

DR. SCOTT: Overworked ER doc who needs a break

Yes, And…

<u>Cast of Characters</u>

BEATRICE: F. College freshman. Undeclared. Home for winter break. Medium to comically zero tap dance skills.

MRS. K: F. Iris Ketchum, is a well-loved, overworked high school theater teacher. Identical twin to SIRI. *Suggest casting the same actor to play both Mrs. K/Iris and twin Mrs. James/Siri.

ADMIN: flexible gender. Inflexible when it comes to district rules and state standards.

TAVEN: (rhymes with raven) flexible gender. High school senior. Zoey's best friend. Raised on Shakespeare but not as intensely as Taven's mom and aunt.

DUKE: M. High school senior, singing delivery person for the family restaurant, Slice of Life. If a Mathlete and a Thespian had a baby and named him after the college where they met. Lovesick over Zoey.

MIRANDA: F. College freshman. Biology major, for now. Laying low during winter break. Translation: shielding herself from the worlds of her stressed-out well-meaning mom as well as her ex best friend, BEATRICE.

HELEN: F. Part-time college freshman. Part-time barista. Part-time dog-sitter. Self-appointed mediator between Beatrice and Miranda.

ZOEY: F. High school senior. Improv is life. The rest is just details. Except for maybe Duke, her once and possibly still crush.

SIRI: F. Mrs. James, Taven's mom, and Iris's identical twin. Don't take Mrs. James' Senior English class unless you want to spend two months studying Shakespeare and plan to earn extra credit by attending the local Renaissance Faire.

PARTYGOERS: 5 or more audience members – DUKE's new friends – all with Happy Birthday cone-hats and "party blower" noisemakers (PARTYGOERS may also include techies and/or cast members from other One acts). Note: Instruct PARTYGOERS to blow their noisemakers whenever a cast member tugs on their ear or they don't have an answer to a question they are asked.

Brillig

AT RISE: Dark stage, as clock chimes eleven.

Scene 1

> A social-emotional support group for college freshmen meeting in a very old small theater.
>
> Voices are heard as ALEX and SADIE approach from opposite sides of the space.

ALEX

Is anyone here?

SADIE

Is that you, Alex?

ALEX

Yeah.

STELLA
(odd ukulele strum)

ALEX

That's got to be Stella.

SADIE

STELLA!!!!!!

(aside)
Ha--I've always wanted to do that.

ALEX
Stop yelling! She's already paranoid. You know that.

STELLA
(ukulele strum)

Never trust darkness.
Evil could be anywhere.
Please turn on the light.

ALEX

It's definitely Stella. She's the only one who talks in haiku.

SADIE
(SADIE smacks into a chair.)

OW!

ALEX

We've got to find a light somewhere.
(Backpack hits metal light.)
I think one just found me.
(More clanking and a single light is illuminated next to an
old trunk.)
It's -- a ghost light.

STELLA

Ghost lights must stay on!
Bad things happen when they're off.
Spirits can harm us.

SADIE

That girl's crazy.

ALEX

Easy there.

SADIE

Is it bad luck if you turn a ghost light back on?

ALEX

Of course not. It's just a light to keep people from injuring themselves or falling off the stage.

SADIE
(Rubs shin.)

It's a little late now.

STELLA

We shouldn't stay here.
Danger lurks in the shadows.
Vibrations are strong.

SADIE

I don't like this.

ALEX
(Sets backpack down.)

Stop it. Both of you. Randall said to meet here so that's what we're going to do. Look. The chairs are all set up.

(Lights up on seven chairs in a semicircle.)

SADIE

Weird. Why are there seven chairs?

(STELLA strums a ukulele chord.)

                          ALEX
Maybe we have new members?

                    (SADIE holds up a mask revealing a skeleton on
                    her hooded sweatshirt.)

                          SADIE
Well, they better get here soon. I have a Halloween party to
get back to, and a monologue to memorize.

                    (The other two stare, surprised.)

                          SADIE
What? Randall says I need to put myself out there. So I'm
putting.

                          ALEX
As a -- who are you supposed to be?

                          SADIE
                         (Bows.)
Endoskeleton.

                          STELLA
Two hundred six bones
Humans take them for granted.
Endoskeleton.

                          SADIE
Why can't you talk like a normal person?

                          ALEX
Leave her alone, Sadie. This is supposed to be a support
group, remember?

4

SADIE

My last support group meeting! Thank you, universe! I get
through this and--

ALEX

What? You're not depressed anymore? It doesn't go away
that easy.

SADIE

Now look who's not being supportive.

> (SADIE pulls out paper to study it; pulls hood of
> sweatshirt on to shut out the world.)

ALEX

Sorry. It's this place. I get that they needed the student center
for the Fall Carnival, but this is creepy.

> (STELLA strums and hums *Stars and Stripes
> Forever*. ALEX reads the words on the trunk.)

ALEX

Wait -- wasn't this the place they shut down after some actor
said Mac-you-know-who on stage?

STELLA

Not the Scottish play!
The MacB-word will curse us.
We need to go NOW.

HILLARY
(off stage voice)

No one's going anywhere.

> (All react as if she's a ghost. HILLARY enters)

                           ALEX

You're not Randall.

                          HILLARY

I'm Hillary. Dr. Randall's not coming tonight, so you lucky
people get me as your facilitator! Let's see –

                   (Refers to her notes.)

Are you Alex?

                           ALEX

Yeah.

                          HILLARY

Sadie?

            (SADIE raises a thumb but keeps studying.)

                          HILLARY

And Stella.

          (STELLA'S answer is a discordant chord on uke.)

                          HILLARY

Nice to meet all of you. No need to worry about an ancient
curse. We're fine. Trust me. That MacB thing is an
Elizabethan PR gimmick to get people to go to the play. This
place is old but it's not haunted. That's nonsense.

                    (No one replies.)

                          HILLARY

Well, OK, since you're wondering, I'm Dr. Randall's
Teaching Assistant. Psychology major, NYU; Psy D in
progress.

ALEX

Where's Randall?

HILLARY

The truth? Probably at home having a glass of wine, after finally getting her hyperactive kids to sleep following a full evening of sugar shock.

ALEX

So you mean she took her twins trick or treating.

HILLARY

Bingo.
                    (sits)
Shall we get started? How can we give each other some support today?

ALEX
                    (sits)
Who are the other chairs for?

HILLARY

No idea. There's no one else on my list. Who would like to share a feeling statement? I'm sure you've done this with Dr. Randall. Just fill in the blanks: I feel _____ because_____.

(No response.)

HILLARY (CONTINUED)
All right. I'll start. I feel confused because no one is
participating. Who wants to go next?
                    (She waits; gets nothing.)
Are there any thoughts you would like to share?

Rest assured everything discussed in the group will be kept
confidential.
        (She has exhausted her facilitator techniques.)
 Whatcha studying, Sadie?

SADIE
Randall says I need activities. So I'm -- there's this play.

HILLARY
That's terrific! What play?

SADIE
Hamlet.
                    (Ghost light flickers.)
The college theater club is doing it. Anyone can audition.

ALEX
Wait. You're gonna be in a play about a depressed guy
contemplating suicide? "TO BE OR NOT TO BE"?

            (Ghost light flickers. STELLA reacts.)

ALEX
You really think that's a good --

HILLARY
Actually, many scholars think Hamlet was the sanest
character in the play.

(Ghost light flickers. STELLA strums in reaction.)

HILLARY
He only pretends to be mad to buy himself some time to make a plan to kill his uncle.

ALEX
I thought you were a psych major?

HILLARY
Sigmund Freud learned a lot from Hamlet.

(Ghost light flickers.)

STELLA
Did you guys see that?
The ghost light is flickering!
I think we should go

ALEX
We can't reschedule. Not with midterms next week.

HILLARY
All right then. What can we say to Stella that might help?

SADIE
Since Randall's not here, could you guys just help with this monologue?

(SADIE goes back to studying.)

HILLARY

Oh, so what I'm hearing is that you would like help with
your monologue.

SADIE

Yeah. That's literally what I just said.

HILLARY

Are you auditioning for Queen Gertrude, Hamlet's mother?

(Ghost light goes crazy. All react.)
Or Ophelia?
(Ghost light. HILLARY tries to ignore it.)
There are all-female Hamlets too, of course, to counteract
the fact that Shakespeare only used male actors back in the
day. Oooh -- Please tell me you're auditioning for the role of
Hamlet. Gives a way different meaning to a lot of the lines:

"O that this too, too solid flesh would melt

Thaw and resolve itself into a dew!"

(beat)
It was my thesis. So much to unpack.

SADIE

Did I mention I have to memorize this monologue for
auditions tomorrow? If I could just --

HILLARY

Of course! We're here for you! Is it something dramatic? I
mean Hamlet is deep.

(Ghost light flickers. STELLA strums.)

HILLARY
Wait. We have a stage right here. Seems like the perfect place to practice for your audition. Go for it.

SADIE
OK. My name is Sadie and my monologue is called —

(ALEX takes a sip from a water bottle. Sadie reads.)

SADIE
Jabberwocky.

(ALEX does a spit take. Hillary shoots ALEX a dirty look.)

HILLARY
So – well -- Sadie -- Good for you for getting involved in stuff on campus. Auditioning is a big step. Your first play, I'm guessing?

(SADIE nods.)

ALEX
This is not what I call supportive. Sadie can't audition for Hamlet –

(Ghost light flickers. All double take.)

ALEX
-- with Jabberwocky! Are you crazy?

HILLARY
(floundering a bit)
Hey, hold on there. No one is crazy. We're all on different journeys. Things can feel…off balance. I mean, everyone's got stuff to deal with. No one is saying --

11

ALEX

I'm saying my high school drama teacher would have boiled you in oil if you chose that for an audition.

(beat)

Jabberwocky? Why? Why? Why?

SADIE

My roommate suggested it.

(STELLA plays a weird chord.)

ALEX

Does she hate you that much?

SADIE

I asked her for something easy. She's auditioning too.

ALEX

That explains a lot.

(STELLA nods.)

HILLARY

Come on, you two. Sadie is allowed to choose Jabberwocky if she wants. I'm sure it's wonderful. And we would love to hear it.

SADIE

But --

HILLARY

We're here for you. Right, friends?

ALEX
(as STELLA strums)

Sure.

SADIE

OK…
(SADIE stands. Takes a deep breath.)
My name is Sadie and I'll be performing Jabberwocky by
Lewis Carroll, from Alice in Wonderland, Through the
Looking Glass.
(SADIE wanders aimlessly, a gesture for each word.)
Twas brillig and the slithy toves

Did gyre--

ALEX
I can't let you do this. Seriously people. It's a nonsense
poem! Gibberish nonsense.

SADIE
I --uh-- actually looked it up online and it's not all gibberish.
A tove is a badger. Some say Brillig means brilliant or shiny,
but according to Humpty Dumpty it refers to 4 o'clock in the
afternoon when people broiled their dinner. Slithy is a
compound of slimy and lithe, meaning active.

ALEX
You looked it up?

SADIE
My roommate always researches her characters when she's
in a play so--

ALEX

So basically, your monologue's about some slimy active badgers. That's "brilliant" all right.

HILLARY

I think it's terrific! You've got this, Sadie. Keep going.

(SADIE tries to continue but panics.)

SADIE

Can I start over?

HILLARY

Of course.

ALEX
(prompting)

'Twas brillig...

SADIE

And the slithy toves did... did...

ALEX

Gyre and gimble in the waves.

(They look at ALEX, surprised.)

ALEX

5th grade, Oral Interp. 2nd place. They docked me points because -- Jabberwocky! I rest my case.

SADIE

I bet they didn't know that gyre and gimble means to bore a hole in something. And, uh, Alex -- it's wabes, not waves. Wabes means the inside of a hill.

14

HILLARY

Maybe that's why you got 2nd place...?

ALEX

So, loosely translated you're saying:
It was early evening
as people were broiling their dinner
And the slimy active badgers
Were boring holes in the hillside?

SADIE

When you put it that way, it does sound pretty dumb.

You're right. I shouldn't do this.

STELLA

You've come way too far
To give up on yourself now.
We believe in you.

SADIE

Thanks, but –

(Crumbles up the paper and tosses it on the floor.)

HILLARY

Maybe Alex will help you find a different one then.

(ALEX reacts. "Me?")

SADIE

No thanks. I'm done. My last meeting folks. It's been real.
Peace out.

(SADIE exits.)

ALEX

Don't look at me. I was just trying to help.

HILLARY

Take it from me. Trying to help doesn't always help. I'm
sure you meant well.

(Door offstage rattles. Pounding.)

SADIE
(off stage)

Are you kidding me?

HILLARY
(calls to SADIE)

What's wrong?

SADIE

Who's got the key?

HILLARY

It can't be locked from the inside.

(HILLARY exits to join SADIE.)

ALEX
(to STELLA)

What?

STELLA
(Sings & strums.)

POP! Goes the weasel.

ALEX

Thanks a lot.
              (STELLA continues to strum.)
Right. I should know better. Every time I try to fix things
they break apart.
                  (beat)
What's the use? I'm outta here too.

              (ALEX exits. The trunk shakes. Or perhaps
              there's a knocking from the inside. Ghost light
              flickers. STELLA's eyes pop.)

STELLA

Hello?

              (STELLA inches her way to the trunk. Ghost
              light flickers. She strums and sings slowly to the
              tune of The Stars and Stripes Forever.)

Be kind to your web-footed friends
For a duck may be somebody's mother.

              (Trunk rumbles increase as STELLA
              approaches.)

Be kind to your friends in the swamp
Where the weather is very very damp.

              (She moves to open the trunk, and sings.)

You might think that this is ... the end.

              (She opens the trunk.)

Well, it is.

17

(STELLA panics as she hears voices:)

OPHELIA (VOICE)
O woe is me! To have seen what I have seen, see what I see!
(audible stretching sound)
The heavens thank thee!

GERTRUDE (VOICE)
The lady doth protest too much, me-thinks.

OPHELIA (VOICE)
You should talk.

(GHOST OF HAMLET'S FATHER rises from
the trunk.)

GHOST
I could a tale unfold whose lightest word would harrow up
thy soul, freeze thy young blood. Make thy two eyes like
stars start from their spheres.

(GHOST lifts a skull from the trunk. Sadie
screams and runs upstage to the exit.)
(BLACKOUT)

18

Scene 2

> The trunk is open, with GHOST and now
> GERTRUDE visible nearby.

OPHELIA (VOICE)
Has she fled?

GERTRUDE
It appears so. She was fine until she saw the skull.
> (to GHOST)
Idiot. How are we going to help anyone if you scare them
away?

GHOST
> (to skull)
Alas, poor Yorick. I knew him, Horatio.

GERTRUDE
That's Hamlet's line.

GHOST
He always got the best ones.

OPHELIA
> (rising from the trunk)
Someone's opened the trunk? We're out of the trunk? We're
out of the trunk!!!

GHOST
On All Hallow's Eve!

OPHELIA

Now all we have to do is--

GERTRUDE

Too bad that handsome cop didn't come back.

OPHELIA

You mean the guy *you* scared away the second he opened the lid?

GERTRUDE

I did no such thing.

GHOST

Why he thought a burglar would be hiding in a musty old trunk is beyond me.

OPHELIA
(to GERTRUDE)
We could have at least helped him catch the perp and gotten out of this mess. But you had to go and try to impress him with your crown.

GERTRUDE

How was I to know he couldn't see us?

OPHELIA

The poor guy thought the crown was floating in midair.

GHOST

We should get started. There's not much time.

(GERTRUDE sits and reads HILLARY's notes aloud.)

GERTRUDE

Social Emotional Therapy Support Group for College
Freshmen. Mission statement: college peer groups can offer
support, improve self-worth, and lessen the stigma of
depression and other conditions.

GHOST

We have found the Holy Grail of people who need fixing.

GHOST	OPHELIA
PEOPLE WHO NEED FIXING!	PEOPLE WHO NEED FIXING!

GERTRUDE

Student 1: Stella, freshman, reclusive tendencies due to
introverted socially phobic helicopter mom.

Student 2: Sadie, freshman, depression due to death of
father.

OPHELIA

Melancholia. I know thee well.

GERTRUDE

Student 3: Alex, freshman, perfectionist, guilt due to parents'
irreconcilable differences and pending divorce.

GHOST

You should be an expert on that one, Gertrude, my love.

GERTRUDE

I am not your love, and please stop calling me Gertrude. It's
enough to be stuck in these roles forever.

GHOST
What would you suggest I call you?

GERTRUDE
We've been in that trunk for how long and you don't know
my real name?

GHOST
Which is…? I feel like I must have known it at some point.

GERTRUDE
Why I'm … my name is … Oh, dear. I've forgotten my own
name.

OPHELIA
All I remember are my lines in the play. Everything else
went blank when the ghost light fell over.

GERTRUDE
Dear me, have I truly been reduced to "ghost of the actor
who played Hamlet's mother"?

GHOST
Try being the ghost of an actor who played a ghost.

OPHELIA
At least you're not stuck as Ophelia. I did not ask to be a
crazy person for eternity. We need to focus, people. You
heard the bells chime eleven. We only have until midnight to
make things right and move on -- finally.

GHOST
Exactly. We need to find closure. Make amends. Fix things.

(HILLARY enters cautiously from UC, with the
others in tow. SADIE, STELLA, and ALEX
have eyes closed or are hiding behind her, afraid
to look.)

GHOST (CONTINUED)
Not flirt with the mortals!

GERTRUDE
You have to admit the cop was cute.

STELLA
Something's in the air.
Voices spinning around us.
The haunting begins.

HILLARY
Hmmm… looks like we have company.

(SADIE, STELLA, ALEX open their eyes.)

Are you here for the support group?

(Jaws of the GHOST, GERTRUDE, and
OPHELIA drop.)

ALEX
Nice Halloween costumes.

OPHELIA
(Singsongs through her smile.)
They can see us.

GERTRUDE
Are you sure? But-?

OPHELIA
Some say All Hallow's Eve lifts the veil between worlds.

GHOST
Time is out of joint. Oh cursed spite.
If ever I was born to set it right.

GERTRUDE
What now?

HILLARY
How about introductions? I'm Hillary. And you are -- ?

GERTRUDE
Oh ... It's been so long.

GHOST
Please call us by our character names. We like to inhabit our
roles -- method acting and all.

OPHELIA
I'm just going to say it. Truth be told, we're –

OPHELIA	GHOST
Ghosts.	Actors!

GHOST
Yes, well, I play the ghost of Hamlet's father. We're here --for
rehearsal. She plays Ophelia. Not a ghost.

GERTRUDE
And I play the beautiful but tragically confused Gertrude.

ALEX

So those aren't Halloween costumes.

GHOST

Correct.

ALEX

And your rehearsal is… here? Right now?

GHOST

Unless you've reserved the space?

HILLARY

I believe Dr. Randall did. We usually don't meet this late but
(gestures at ALEX)
Alex had a night class.

GHOST

One must use whatever time we are given.

HILLARY

I guess we were double-booked. Our session should be over
by midnight though.

OPHELIA

But that's too late!

GHOST

What she means is... perhaps we can help you now. It will
give us something to do until rehearsal starts.

HILLARY

Of course, you need the rest of the cast.

GHOST

What can we do? Please.

(OPHELIA digs in the trunk, gives GERTRUDE her crown.)

GERTRUDE

Thank you. I was wondering where that went.

OPHELIA

Huzzah! I'm helping.
(to GHOST)
Do you feel that? We're here to help them with unfinished business.

SADIE
(Thinking about a quick escape.)
Great. I have a party to get back to. See ya.

OPHELIA

Oh no, you don't. Sit. What's *your* problem? We're fixing it NOW.

(SADIE sits but won't engage. OPHELIA turns to ALEX.)

You there. What's in the backpack? Unfinished homework?

ALEX
(Rattled, digs in backpack, guilty.)
Uh. I didn't finish my lunch today. I have half a sandwich and a pickle --?

OPHELIA

Real food!

(OPHELIA dives for the sandwich but GHOST
stops her.)

GHOST

We can't. That is to say, we shouldn't. To quote the Bard,
"Most dear actors eat no -- half sandwiches nor pickles -- for
we are to utter sweet breath." But many thanks.

(Beat, OPHELIA gets the message.)

HILLARY

Actually, since you're clearly well-seasoned actors, Sadie
needs a monologue for her Hamlet audition. Could you help
with that?

(OPHELIA pulls a bouquet of dried flowers out
of the trunk and gives them to SADIE.)

OPHELIA

My flowers! Perfect. You can do my graveyard monologue.
Repeat after me, Sadie.

(Gestures for SADIE to give rosemary to
STELLA.)

There's rosemary, that's for remembrance. Pray you love,
remember.

(OPHELIA stares at SADIE until she gives the
rosemary to STELLA and repeats:)

SADIE

...remember.

OPHELIA

(gestures for SADIE to give pansies to ALEX)

There's pansies, that's for thoughts.

(OPHELIA pulls SADIE out of her chair.
SADIE gives pansies to ALEX.)

SADIE

For thoughts.

ALEX

Thanks?

(Pace picks up as OPHELIA gestures, and
SADIE tries to keep up while distributing
flowers and repeating:)

OPHELIA
(to GHOST)
There's fennel for you. And columbines.
(to GERTRUDE)
There's rue for you and some for me.
We may call it Herb of Grace o'Sundays.
(to herself and the stage.)
Oh, how I've missed this.
(to GERTRUDE)
You must wear your rue with a difference.

GERTRUDE

How many times do I have to apologize?

OPHELIA

(to SADIE, with kindness)

There's a daisy. I would give you some violets

SADIE & OPHELIA

but they withered all when my father died.

SADIE

They say he made a good end.

(beat)

I'm not sure where that came from.

OPHELIA

'Tis a gift.

HILLARY

That was lovely, Sadie.

ALEX

Except she can't use a monologue from the play she's
auditioning for.

(GERTRUDE finds a dagger covered with stage
blood in the trunk.)

GERTRUDE

How about Lady Macbeth? "Give ME the daggers. I'll do it
then."

SADIE

You said the MacB word on stage. That's the curse that closed this theater down!

OPHELIA

That's... not what happened.

(points at GERTRUDE)
She turned the ghost light off!

GERTRUDE

It was an accident!

STELLA
(shudders)

It is not safe here.
There has to be a stage door.
It's our only hope!

(She grabs ALEX and SADIE and they exit.
HILLARY starts to follow.)

GHOST

Don't go. Please!

(GHOST, OPHELIA and GERTRUDE stare
hopefully at a suspicious HILLARY.)

There has to be something we can help you with.
Immediately, if not sooner. We're in a bit of a hurry.

HILLARY

You can start by telling me how you guys got in here.

GHOST

It's a long story.

OPHELIA

No it's not. We came in through the stage door.

HILLARY

So there is another way out!

(HILLARY exits toward the stage door.)

GHOST

Terrific. You know that stage door has been bricked up for years.

OPHELIA

Well, what was I supposed to say? Gee, decades ago we were moving that trunk and Gertrude here knocked over the ghost light and that's the last thing we remember?

GERTRUDE

Here we go again. Let's blame Gertrude.

HILLARY
(Reenters.)
There's no way you got in through that stage door.

(The other three return with her.)

Who are you anyway?

STELLA

They're ghosts. Aren't you?

(ALEX and SADIE double take to STELLA.)

GHOST

Well, I am -- like I said.

STELLA

All of you are.

(beat)
You couldn't eat the sandwich. You don't have names. You came from the trunk!

SADIE

Stella -- That wasn't a haiku.

(A moment as each of them stomps, taps out the beat, or uses their fingers to count the syllables of what STELLA just said.)

ALL

All of you are. You couldn't eat the sandwich. You don't have names. You came from the trunk!

ALEX

Sadie's right. Too many syllables.
(beat)
Wait --You guys are ghosts? For real?

HILLARY

That's impossible.

GHOST

So what if we are? You think you've got problems? You think you need support? We have to help make things right or we go back in that trunk at midnight. AGAIN!

GERTRUDE

No!
                    (Desperate; trying a new tactic.)
"If we shadows have offended,
Think but this and all is mended
That you have but slumbered here
While these visions did appear."

                    (GERTRUDE claps her hands hopefully.
                    Nothing happens. She claps again.)

OPHELIA

What are you doing?

GERTRUDE

It worked for Puck. "Give me your hands if we be friends."
Everybody claps and poof, he disappears!

OPHELIA

That's a good monologue for you, Sadie. Midsummer Night's
Dream.

SADIE

Forget it. I'm not an actor. Who am I kidding? I should join a
book club or something.

GERTRUDE

Acting is pretending. Everyone does that.
                    (to ALEX)
You're pretending. Aren't you?

ALEX

NO.

STELLA

Yes. Alex pretends to be perfect.

ALEX

That's ridiculous.

GERTRUDE

Well, you're right about that. We've been around long enough to know nobody's perfect.

HILLARY

Parents, especially. It's not your job to keep them together.

ALEX

Is that what Randall told you?
(to STELLA)
At least I don't talk in haikus!

STELLA

Maybe I want people to leave me alone. Is that so bad?
(to GHOST)
Aren't you guys here to help?

GHOST

"There is nothing either good nor bad, but thinking makes it so."

HILLARY

Do you have the entire script of Hamlet memorized?

GHOST

You hang around backstage for rehearsals of an entire play five nights a week for months on end, and you'll have every line memorized too.

SADIE

So you aren't here for rehearsal?

OPHELIA

We have been these characters forever! Please help us. I'm so sick of being stuck.

SADIE

I feel you.

OPHELIA

You do?

SADIE

It's my last session so I might as well say it. I'm sad, OK? And so mad! But that doesn't make me crazy! How would you feel if you were in class 3,000 miles away from home and your "perfect" little brother texts you: Dad died?

OPHELIA

Disbelieving. Distraught. Devastated.

HILLARY

Of course. Those are very valid feelings.

SADIE

An hour later my stepmom calls. Do I get a shoulder to cry on? Urgent requests to "Come home quick." No. She doesn't want to interrupt my studies. They knew he was sick months before and they didn't want to tell me.

OPHELIA

I'm so sorry.

SADIE

Then after his "Celebration of Life" everyone expected me to
be OK. Like *poof!* he's gone. Get over it. I tried, I really did,
but I got tired of pretending. Except being not-OK is
exhausting too. I thought this group would help.

(They look at HILLARY.)

HILLARY

Let's all take a deep breath.

(Only OPHELIA & HILLARY do this.)

SADIE

Wait. If you really are ghosts, could you maybe talk to my
dad for me? Please? I never got to say goodbye.

GHOST

It doesn't exactly work that way.

SADIE

Well then how does it work?

GHOST

If we knew we wouldn't be here.

SADIE

I thought you were here to help!

(They look at HILLARY again.)

HILLARY

And another deep breath!
(beat)
I wish I could help. I do. I'm … pretending I know what I'm
doing, actually.

ALEX

How's that working so far?

HILLARY

I told Dr. Randall that I'm quitting the program. I'm as
messed up as anyone else. How am I supposed to help
people?
(beat)

OPHELIA

(OPHELIA picks up crumpled JABBERWOCKY and reads.)

Twas brillig and the slithy toves
Did gyre and gimble in the wabes
Why does that sound familiar?

ALEX

It's a nonsense poem by Lewis Carroll, from Through the
Looking Glass.

OPHELIA

No, I've heard those rhythms, that cadence, somewhere else
before.

GHOST

Horatio says it in Hamlet, Act I, scene 1.

OPHELIA

That's it!

GHOST

"The graves stood tenantless, and the sheeted dead
Did squeak and gibber in the Roman streets."

ALEX

Whoa.

OPHELIA

Heaven and earth, I LOVED THIS STAGE. My place to be
me. Or someone else entirely. Not the someone others
expected me to be.

SADIE

I told you it's not all nonsense.

OPHELIA

My graveyard monologue sounds like nonsense to some, you
know.
(Epiphany.)

ALEX

Ophelia couldn't have been totally mad if she knew how to
match the flowers' meanings to the characters' feelings.

OPHELIA

Ophelia knows what she's doing. She's not crazy! She gives
rue to Gertrude because she should be regretting her hasty
marriage to her dead husband's brother.

(They all look at GERTRUDE.)

GERTRUDE
Don't look at me. That's Shakespeare's twisted mind!

(OPHELIA hands SADIE the poem.)

GHOST
(to SADIE, encouraging her)
Speak the speech I pray you.
Pronounce it trippingly on the tongue.

SADIE
(over-gesturing as before)
Twas brillig and the slithy toves
Did gyre and gimble in the wabes

(GHOST stops SADIE, patiently coaching.)

GHOST
Do not saw the air too much with your hands thus
But use all gently ... give it smoothness

GERTRUDE
Be not too tame neither.

SADIE
(louder, SADIE tries strutting around)
All mimsy were the borogoves,
And the mome raths outgrabe.

GERTRUDE
Yet do not strut nor bellow.

SADIE
(getting the hang of it now)
Beware the Jabberwock, my son!
The jaws that bite, the claws that catch!
Beware the Jubjub bird, and shun
The frumious Bandersnatch!

GHOST
(encouraging)
Suit the action to the word, the word to the action.

GERTRUDE
Pretend the Bandersnatch is your brother. The Jubjub bird is
your stepmom. And the Jabberwock, your sadness.

ALEX
Method acting, right?

GERTRUDE
Brillig, my dear.

(SADIE's stage combat intensifies. All watch
SADIE vs an invisible foe.)

GHOST
Atta, girl!

(GHOST moves upstage, backing into the
shadows as SADIE advances for the final attack.
Her movement takes her further downstage as
the others gather around and watch in awe.)

SADIE
One two, one two, and through and through!

(Beat. SADIE's catharsis is visible.)

OPHELIA

This is marvelous. I could stay in this moment forever.

GERTRUDE
(To Ophelia)

Over my dead body.
(Stella laughs momentarily but stops herself.)
Stick to the plan!

OPHELIA

Look around.

(deep breath)

Really look.

STELLA
(Cross to trunk.)

Who knew a bunch of ghosts could help me more than eight
sessions with Dr. Randall?
(Gets skull out of trunk.)
Also, hanging out with all you weirdos is way better than
being by myself.

OPHELIA

I was a loner too, back then. And lonely.

(beat)

Why are all of us so afraid to live while we have the
chance?

ALEX

Good question.

STELLA

They say you need the dark to appreciate the light.
(as if skull is speaking)
Maybe a little madness is OK.

HILLARY

Maybe we're not supposed to fix everything.

ALEX
(to HILLARY)

Or know how.

STELLA
(With a quiet laugh.)

We can barely fix ourselves.

GHOST (VOICE)

Adieu, Adieu.

(All look for GHOST, who has disappeared.)

SADIE

No -- wait!

GHOST (VOICE)

Remember me.

SADIE

I will! Oh my -- I will. Always. -- Thank you!
If you do see my dad…

(beat)

Right. It probably doesn't work that way.

HILLARY

Maybe you could talk to him, Sadie. Here. Now.

(OPHELIA backs into the shadows & exits
during the following.)

SADIE

(Beat. Takes a deep breath. Softly:)
I love you, Dad.

(Louder now.)
Forty thousand brothers could not with all their quantity of
love make up my sum!

OPHELIA (VOICE)

Oh my. … Can't I stay? Start over? Live?

GERTRUDE

'Tis our time. Sweets to the sweet! Farewell.

STELLA

Ophelia's gone!

(The clock begins to chime twelve.)

GERTRUDE

You've released us.

(BLACKOUT)

Scene 3

> (Ghosts are gone. The others take a moment to process this. STELLA strums & hums *Row, Row, Row Your Boat*.)

STELLA

Maybe life *is* but a dream…

SADIE

"Ay -- There's the rub."

ALEX
(To SADIE)
How do you suddenly know all those lines from Hamlet?

STELLA

Ophelia said it was a gift.

ALEX

Yeah, uh -- I wouldn't tell anyone that outside of this group.

SADIE

"Though this be madness, there is method in it."

STELLA

What would you do if you could start over? Really live --like Ophelia said.

HILLARY

That sounds scary.

STELLA

We don't have to start with anything big.

(STELLA strums.)

ALEX

I always wanted to play the ukulele.

STELLA

I can teach you.

ALEX

Really?

(STELLA strums and nods.)

SADIE

Will you guys be here next week?

ALEX

Wait. You're coming back to the group? But I thought that this was your last meeting.

SADIE

Maybe I just like having friends.

ALEX

You should come back too, Hillary. Even if Randall's here.

HILLARY

O ... K.

SADIE

And let's meet here. In this theater, from now on. It needs us. All of us. Don't you feel it?

STELLA

I do.

                          SADIE

This stage needs people. And laughter. And sadness. And
madness.

                    LOCKSMITH (VOICE)

Did someone call a locksmith?

                          HILLARY

We're in here!

                    LOCKSMITH (VOICE)

Yeah well I'm not coming in. There's nothing wrong with the
front door. Y'all should get out of there. The place is
haunted!

                          HILLARY

Ha--that's crazy!

                    (They start to exit as SADIE goes to turn off the
                    ghost light.)

                    HILLARY, STELLA, ALEX

NO!!!!!

                          SADIE

Just kidding.

                    (Lights lower to leave only the ghost light
                    illuminated as the others exit upstage together.
                    SADIE closes the trunk. Speaks to the
                    universe.)

Good night, sweet friends.

And flights of angels sing thee to thy rest.

(Ghost light remains on. SADIE exits.)

<u>CURTAIN</u>

What Light?

SETTING: A slow night in the Emergency
Department of a university hospital, on a snowy
evening in late November. The stage is separated
into three sections, as in three exam rooms.

AT RISE: All is quiet except for a soft but
excruciating cacophony of moaning from JAKE
Room 2 (C.), an occasional OW from LUCY,
and frustrated, audible sighs percussing from
FINN in Room 1.

Lights up only on Room 2 (C) and JAKE curled
up in fetal position, moaning while a NURSE
sets up an IV. As little focus as possible on
LUCY in Room 1 (R). holding her wrist above
her heart and FINN sitting up, head wrapped in a
bloody towel, in Room 3 (L). Note: Patients are
in street clothes. No hospital gowns needed until
Scene 7.)

Scene 1: Big Break

NURSE

Good news, Jake!

(Cacophony simmers on low at the sound of the
NURSE.)

The doctor says we can rule out any serious abdominal
injury. These meds should help.

JAKE

What about my heart?

                    NURSE
You'll get over her. Meanwhile
                         (Pats the IV)
Have some fluids.

             (JAKE groans. NURSE exits to Room 1 to see
             to LUCY.)

                    LUCY
               (holding her wrist)
Ow, Ow, Ow!!!! Son of a -- .

                    NURSE
Now, now. No foul language please.

                    LUCY
OW. (beat) Sorry.

                    NURSE
               (with clipboard)
On a scale of one to ten, what number would you say your
pain is right now, LUCY? One: ingrown toenail. Ten: you're
birthing triplets without an epidural.

                    LUCY
Try a thousand, maybe????
                    (winces)
Fobbing rump-fed maggot pie!

                    NURSE
A thousand...?
             (Adds note to chart.)
I see...

                    LUCY
I'm serious. This was my big break!

NURSE

I know it feels that way, my friend. As a nurse, I can't
actually give you a diagnosis…but it might just be a fracture.

LUCY
(to her wrist)

Mangled joithead!

NURSE

Would you like me to get you something for the—

LUCY

YES. Can you get me OUT of here? Please? We open
tonight.
What time is it? Oh no, No, NO, it's almost -- Curtain -—
please? I need to--

NURSE

 Well, we usually keep the curtains closed, for privacy,
but, if you insist.

> (NURSE opens curtain between LUCY &
> JAKE, who sits up, his moaning morphing to a
> **whoa** as he sees LUCY.)

The doctor should be here soon.

LUCY

You don't understand. It's my first college production
Romeo and Juliet! They don't usually cast a freshman in the

_____.

> (About to say Fall Production, but JAKE and
> possibly the audience think she's going to say
> Lead.)

OW!!!!

(NURSE wraps ice pack around LUCY'S wrist as a temporary splint.)

NURSE

This should help. I'm going to take you down the hall to Imaging. The doctor will want x-rays before it's clear if you need a cast or surgery.

(They exit. Lights up on Room 2 as JAKE watches her go.)

JAKE
(to the universe.)

I'd cast her …a million times …What's that line? "But soft… what light through yonder breaks? It is the sun -- and Juliet is… Juliet is…"

(moans)

FINN (VOICE)

The moon.

JAKE

(To the voice next door, or possibly still the universe.)

Are you sure? That doesn't sound right.

(Lights up to half in Room 3 as they talk through the curtain between them.)

FINN

I think so. We had to read it in 7th grade.

JAKE

Shakespeare 1A here. The professor made us do scenes.
(beat) Uh--I don't think Juliet's the moon. It makes you
wonder too much. Like half-moon? Full moon?
(moans)

RA
(enters Room 3)

She's the sun, my Bard-bungling friends. "It is the East and
Juliet is the -—"

FINN

Great.

RA

Nice to see you too, Finn.

FINN

What are you doing here?

RA

Would you rather talk to the campus cop?

(BLACKOUT)

Scene 2: Break-up

(NURSE enters Room 3, ever smiling, checks
FINN's chart. RA sits in visitor's chair.)

NURSE

Sorry you've had to wait so long, Elizabeth.

FINN

It's Finn.

NURSE

And I'm Nurse Sunny! Well, that's what they call me
anyway. It started as a joke, but I like it. Nice to meet you,
Elizabeth Finn. We're a bit understaffed, so--.

FINN

My name is Finn. I go by my last name.

NURSE

Finn?

JAKE

Finn? Sunny? "What's in a name? A rose by any other
name–"

FINN
(grumbling at curtain / JAKE)

Very funny.

(NURSE smiles and proceeds to remove the
bloody towel, very carefully as some places are
stuck, through the following.)

NURSE

Oh I get it. That's Shakespeare. You are funny! I'll be
with you in a minute.

JAKE

Thanks.

FINN
(To RA)

So, anyway, you should go. Stress isn't good for me. I might
have a concussion. No bright lights, or—

NURSE
(Towel removed, she examines the injury.)

Goodness. We're going to need to irrigate this wound.

RA
(To NURSE)

Do you need me to go?
(Simultaneously)

FINN:	NURSE:
YES!	NO. The more the merrier, I always say!

FINN

Don't I have any say? Ahhh-OWWWW.

NURSE

Easy there.
(aside to RA)

I gave your sister something for the pain, which should be
kicking in about now.

RA

Oh, Finn's not my sister. I'm the Resident Advisor.

                              FINN
Lucky me.

                               RA
Come on, Finn, I'm here to help, not make things worse.

                             NURSE
This might sting.

                              FINN
HOLY mother of OW!
                      (JAKE moans.)

                             NURSE
Try to relax.
                (Puts pillow behind FINN's head.)
That's it. I'll be back in a minute.
                      (Exits with towel)

                               RA
So, are you ready to tell me what happened?

                 (JAKE moans from next door.)

                              FINN
Here? With Romeo listening next door?

                              JAKE
Forget I exist. Everyone else does.

                              FINN
Says the guy who's not listening.

                    JAKE
Says the guy with the broken heart. Who's dying, by the
way, because his girlfriend of three years — the only reason
I chose to attend the university closest to hers — recently
and lovingly informed me I've been replaced by a Theta-
freaking-frat boy. Happy Thanksgiving break to me.
                    (moans)

                    FINN
That sucks.

                    RA
Agree.

                    FINN
We agree on something?

                    RA
November break-ups happen all the time. High school
girlfriend, right?

                    JAKE
Uh —- yeah.
                    (sighs)
Rosalyn.

                    RA
Separate colleges. New friends. New relationships. "Love
the one you're with…"

                    FINN
                    (to RA)
How is this helpful?

                              RA

You meet up back home at Thanksgiving – you can't wait to
see her, hold her, and BOOM.

                             FINN
                  (The meds are kicking in.)
BOOM!

                              RA

(Now reminiscing about a very similar personal experience.)
HE "needs space." You've "grown apart." And you wanna
know WHY he had this SUDDEN epiphany? HE realized he
didn't want to give you a Christmas present!!!! A Christmas
present??? I'm Jewish!!!!

                             FINN
BOOM ba da BOOM BOOM!

                             JAKE
Uh — sorry?

                              RA
We celebrate LIGHT.

                             FINN
                     (feeling no pain)
"But soft... what light through yonder window breaks?"

                              RA
TWO years and that was his reasoning?

                             JAKE
Three years actually. Ros and I met at our high school
orientation. Freshman year. It was love at first sight. Well,
for me, anyway. We were juniors when she finally gave me a
chance.

FINN

How does LIGHT break a window?

NURSE
(enters Room 2/ check JAKE's chart)
Feeling any better, JAKE?

FINN

No, no, no. His name is Romeo.

JAKE

Me?

NURSE

OK Romeo. When's the last time you had a bowel
movement?

JAKE

WHAT?
(Knowing FINN can hear.)
Listen -- can we use our inside voices here?

NURSE

Of course!
(She doesn't.)
Have you been hydrating?

JAKE

Do canned caffeinated beverages count?

NURSE

Nope. Fruit or fiber?

JAKE

Pepperoni pizza? (beat) That's not my usual but they didn't
have pineapple.

NURSE
(Still smiling)
And your last poop was?

JAKE
(moans)
YOU'RE KILLING ME.

NURSE
(Still smiling!)
That's all you, friend. Caffeine, processed grains. No fruits or fiber -– no

JAKE
Shi--

NURSE
Keep it clean, Romeo.

JAKE
POOP!

NURSE
That's the goal.

JAKE
But my heart.

NURSE
You've got the heart of an --

JAKE
Ex. That's how she introduced me to her frat boy. "This is my EX." I swear, my heart disintegrated.

FINN

"Swear not by the moon —— the constipated moon!"

NURSE
(bursts into laughter)

Sorry.

(To FINN))

That was good. Except,no. This is no time to joke. The pain
is real, I know.

(Gets it together again. Gives JAKE a pill
[laxative] via paper cup & glass of water.)

But there's a simple solution. Bottoms up.

(FINN cracks up.)

NURSE

Just give it time.

(BLACKOUT)

Scene 3:Break-in
(Room 3)

FINN
(To RA)
Are you still here? "Good night, good night! Partying is such sweet sorrow!"

RA
It's **parting**. She's saying she doesn't want Romeo to leave.

FINN
YOU can go though. You're my RA.

RA
Yes, I am.

FINN
Wait --
(confused)
Are we at the dorm?

RA
We're in the ER. At the hospital. You were injured.

FINN
(remembering)
Phoebe hit me! With her lacrosse stick! You should be arresting her, officer.

RA
No one is arresting anyone. Although breaking and entering —

FINN

I didn't break anything! She never locks her door. Whoooo
does that? Was she born in a convent?

RA

So... OK, technically you didn't break in. But you entered.

> (Lights remain low as NURSE wheels LUCY
> back to Room 1 to rest.)

FINN

She had my notes! MY notes.
> (Looks around for them.)
My NOTES!

RA

According to Phoebe, those notes are hers.

FINN

HA. They could have been. Half hers, anyway, if she'd
actually done her part of the research.

RA

Go on.

> (NURSE returns to room 3 and proceeds to
> temporarily bandage FINN's head wound during
> the following.)

FINN

I hate it when professors make you team up for a project
and only one of you does the work.

NURSE

Well, that's certainly not the Girl Scout way.

RA

And you're saying you—

FINN

Did all the work!

NURSE

Easy, there.

FINN

Only Phoebe insisted on using her fancy computer. And she had lacrosse practice. And our paper was due.
(realization)
Today.

NURSE

This should help until we get some stitches in that. The Doctor will be along to check it soon.
(Sighs –still smiling somehow)
Oh, who am I kidding? We're short-staffed and the Doctor is with some way sicker patient than you all.
(laughs)
And snow's piling up outside.
(Cheerier than ever.)
We're never getting out of here.

FINN

But my English paper! You can discharge me, right?

NURSE

Sorry. No. The Doc's gonna need to suture that laceration.

FINN
(To RA)
Can you go get the notes? I was printing them out when she clobbered me. Please? I need that grade.

NURSE

You'd better hurry.

RA

I want to believe you.

FINN

Go get the notes and I'll prove it to you. I bet my way-too-busy "study partner" Phoebe doesn't even know what it's about! Go ask her why they say "Break a Leg" in the theater!

NURSE
(raises hand)

It's good luck!

LUCY

Breaking your leg maybe. Breaking a wrist -— not so much.

FINN

I cover four theories in my — "our"— paper. Theory number one: in ancient Greece, audiences stomped their feet like crazy if they liked the play--instead of applauding.

NURSE

Goodness me.
(delighted)
You could BREAK your leg that way!

FINN

Number two—

NURSE
(Calls to next door.)
That's my wish for you, Romeo.

JAKE

Terrific. A dump to recover from a dump.

LUCY
(laughing)

You're disgusting.

JAKE

You're beautiful. Is that a balcony injury?

LUCY

Volleyball dig.
(To her wrist.)
Jarring guts-gripping bum-bailey.

JAKE

Where did you learn to curse like a--

LUCY

Bawdy tickle-brained harpy?

JAKE

Took the words right out of my mouth.

LUCY

The director taught us Shakespearean slang. So if we drop a
line, we can always curse.

NURSE

Constipated patient falls for a pretty, potty-mouth Juliet! It's
a match made in heaven.

JAKE

If this nurse thing doesn't pan out, you could try stand-
up.

LUCY
(to JAKE)
Listen, I'm not --

FINN
In Shakespeare's day, audiences who liked the play banged their chairs on the ground—

NURSE
Wait a second. Chairs have legs! That can break…

LUCY AND JAKE:
(to RA)
GO get those notes!

(RA exits.)

FINN
Number three—

JAKE
Uh, Nurse? I gotta --

(Optional fart SFX.)

(BLACKOUT)

Scene 4: Break Dance

(Curtains between the exam rooms are open
now. Camaraderie is contagious.)

NURSE

Jake, my boy, you're free to go, as soon as the doctor -—

LUCY

There IS no doctor, is there? It's like the Tooth Fairy or --
Little Mermaid on Ice. Impossible stuff adults make up to
give you hope.

FINN

Actually, experts say that the Vikings were the first to give
their teeth to the tooth fairy. They believed children's teeth
were good luck. They carried them into battle.

JAKE

More kernels of knowledge from that Luck and Literature
class?

FINN

The very same one I'm about to fail. Thank you for the
reminder, Romeo. I bet my study partner Phoebe can't tell
you that the modern Tooth Fairy is from a play by Ester
Watkins.

LUCY

His name is Jake. Why do you keep calling him Romeo?

JAKE

No idea.

FINN

"A rose by any other name…"

(JAKE & FINN laugh.)

LUCY

Wait. You're laughing at ME. You KNOW, don't you? And now you're having a good old time making jokes?

FINN AND JAKE

No jokes.

JAKE

I swear.

NURSE

Scouts honor.

JAKE

Finn Elizabeth over there called me Romeo when I said...I bet you're the best Juliet ever.

FINN

I hate you.

NURSE

Know *what*?

LUCY

That I'm not—

JAKE

"Two of the fairest stars in all the heaven, do --" something something... Shoot. What's that line?

LUCY

Romeo says that about Juliet's eyes.

JAKE

Perfect.

(LUCY starts crying.)

FINN

What's wrong? I think he meant it as a compliment.

LUCY

I'm not... The play's halfway over by now.

FINN

This is your fault, Romeo.

JAKE

"The fault, dear Finn, is not in our stars…"

NURSE

THE FAULT IN OUR STARS. I loved that book. (beat) She dies… of cancer.

(LUCY & NURSE cry together during the following.)

NURSE

No—I can't cry. I won't. Oh no, no—I am…

LUCY

It's OK. Let it out.

NURSE

(shakes her head vigorously)

No—I can't --I have to be cheerful. I see too much sadness. Too much pain. Too much loss. If I cry, I won't stop.

(Crying escalates)

                    FINN
                  (to JAKE)
DO something, you idiot.

                    JAKE
Like what?

          (FINN gestures anything but it looks like she's
          trying to dance.)

                    JAKE
WHAT? Oh, no. I'm not—

          (More frantic gestures from FINN that he thinks
          means break dancing.)

                    JAKE
OK, but you have to beat-box.

          (Jake starts his not-very-good break dancing.
          FINN tries to beat-box. NURSE and LUCY
          stop, incredulous. He gets them to join
          in,dancing, with an occasional "Go Romeo!"
          from the NURSE combined with OW! from
          LUCY.)

               VOICE / DOCTOR
WHAT'S GOING ON HERE?

          (BLACKOUT)

Scene 5: Break It Up

NURSE
(still dancing)

Doctor Scott!

DOCTOR

Have you all gone mad? I've just finished an eight-hour shift to learn we're snowed in and find a dance party in ER?

FINN

"Partying is such sweet sorrow…"

(JAKE & LUCY try not to laugh.)

NURSE

Dancing is pretty therapeutic.
(To JAKE)
I needed that. Thanks.
(To DOC)
You should try it.

DOCTOR

Not in my ER. Not after the day I've had.

NURSE

Who says ER can't be cheery? Patients are scared enough when they get here! I tell myself each morning: If you're going to rise, you might as well shine!

DOCTOR
(sternly)

NURSE SUNNY!
(beat)
May I speak to you for a moment?

NURSE
(She sobers.)

Of course.

(They exit.)

JAKE

Uh-oh. She's in trouble.

FINN

SHE's in trouble? I'm up for entering-without-the-breaking, and currently flunking Luck and Literature!

LUCY

That's not true. Your RA will help. That's what they do.

JAKE

And you'll get your cast on, FINN will get their head examined,
(He laughs.)

FINN

Watch it, Buddy.

JAKE

And we'll all go home…and

LUCY

We'll never see each other again.

JAKE

Or… I was thinking… we could go see you in the play. Well, I could.

FINN

I'm down for that. Romeo and Juliet here we come.

LUCY

NO.

JAKE

No?

LUCY

I mean—my understudy probably did such a good job; they
probably gave her my part. Permanently.

JAKE

They wouldn't do that.

LUCY

I might have a huge cast on my arm—and

JAKE

The show must go on!

FINN

We'll go and complain.

JAKE

We'll demand to see our Juliet!

LUCY

You guys! Stop!
                    (about to cry again.)

LUCY

You can't.

NURSE
                    (enters)
Jake? Let's get you discharged.
                    (Tries not to laugh)

74

NURSE (CONTINUED)

No pun intended.

JAKE

Perfect.

(NURSE & JAKE exit.)

FINN

And then there were two. (beat) What's up with you, anyway?

LUCY

I –blew it with Jake. (beat) Plus you guys don't want to come to the play. Trust me.

FINN

Are you kidding me? That guy would go see you if you were the spear carrier in Act 3.

LUCY

He thinks I'm Juliet. And now I'll never see him again…

FINN

That's it, isn't it? You're a spear carrier.

LUCY

(beat) I'm the nurse.
(Weeping/ breaks down)
I tried to tell him. I'm not the lead. I'm a freshman, so actually NURSE is a great part. But my eyes aren't the fairest stars—I wear a padded suit with giant boobs and say "Marry" a lot. And "alas the day!" and so many Anons I get them mixed up.

FINN
(laughs)
The NURSE!!!That's super-cool!

NURSE
Yes--coming! What's wrong???

FINN
(Hugs LUCY)
I can't wait to see you!

DOCTOR
Nurse—prep Lucy for her cast. Let's look at that head,
Elizabeth.

LUCY
The name is Finn.

(As they go to their original exam rooms.)

FINN
(yells)
Jake won't care, you idiot. As long as he can be your Romeo.

(BLACKOUT)

Scene 6: Take a Break

FINN

And then there was one.

> (FINN Exits, ostensibly though the waiting
> room — or outside — head bandaged. Sees
> JAKE sitting there.)

Make that two.

JAKE

How's it going?

FINN

Oh, you know. Nothing that a few stitches couldn't fix.

JAKE

You can appeal your grade, you know. Go talk to your
professor. When they see you're actually injured...

FINN

Thanks. Maybe I will. (beat) Lucy likes you, you know.

JAKE

So you don't think I'm an idiot for waiting around...?

FINN

Oh I'm pretty sure you're an idiot, but you guys should ...
talk.

JAKE

It's too late. I blew it.

FINN

Lucy said the same thing.

JAKE

Yeah, sure she did. I —— should go.

FINN

If you say so.

(They start to exit in different directions.)

See you around —— or not.

(They are just about off.)

Parting is such sweet sorrow.

(JAKE exits first. Lights lower as this scene ends, or so we think.)

JAKE
(offstage)

Why doesn't she want us to go to the play?

FINN
(stops)

You'll have to ask her.

JAKE
(enters)

I'm asking you.

(They step closer with each line, as lights come back up, through the following.)

Is she worried I'm just rebounding from Rosalyn? Because I'm not. I know I fall fast, but she's --

                              FINN
She isn't who you think she is.

                              JAKE
OK...(beat) illuminate me.

                              FINN
She isn't Juliet. In the play.

                              JAKE
That's it?

                              FINN
She tried to tell you. She didn't want to disappoint you.

                              JAKE
                           (elated)
I don't care if she's not Juliet. I'm a little pissed at the director –or whoever cast her —— as --?

                              FINN
The nurse.

                              JAKE
I bet she's the best nurse ever.

                              FINN
You could still be her Romeo.

                              JAKE
That's it! (grabs FINN's arm) Come on!

                         (BLACKOUT)

Scene 7: Break a Leg

(RA Enters with cross-country skis & poles
she's used to get there in the blizzard.)

RA

Am I too late? Where's Finn?

NURSE:

Huzzah! You're just in time. Oooh! And aren't you some sort
of Shakespearean scholar?

RA

Me? No. I'm pre-law. And Finn's RA.

NURSE

But you know some Romeo and Juliet lines, right?

RA

I guess.

NURSE

Hey, Finn! Come quick!

(FINN enters, a hospital gown rearranged and
belted as a tunic.)

FINN

Sunny! Get yourself a costume. The Doctor's almost done.

(NURSE exits. FINN sees RA)

OII!

RA

Finn--I couldn't find the hard copy of your notes.

FINN

Oh.

RA

But I went to your professor and told her what happened.

FINN

Oh.

RA

I told her you practically had your entire essay memorized, and you were stuck in ER so I hoped she would accept the essay Phoebe turned in—for both of you.

FINN

You did?

RA

And I suggested she question Phoebe on the key points.

FINN

Thank you!!!

(FINN hugs RA)

RA

You're…welcome.

FINN

And now we need you in the play.

RA

What play?

NURSE

You'll see. Hide!

(FINN pulls RA aside and they hide. DOCTOR and LUCY enter, her arm in a cast & sling.)

DOCTOR

I'll see you in three weeks then, Lucy.

LUCY

Thanks. (beat) Are Jake and Finn still here?

(The DOCTOR has left. LUCY looks around, but JAKE and FINN are gone. She starts to leave.)

NURSE

(runs in)

Lucy—don't go! What's that famous Juliet line? "Oh Romeo, Romeo—"

LUCY

"Wherefore art thou Romeo?"

NURSE

Yes!

(She giggles)

What comes next?

LUCY

"Deny thy father and refuse thy name or if thou wilt not—"

(JAKE enters, dressed as Romeo -- somehow.)

JAKE

"Be but sworn my love and I'll no longer be a Montague."

RA
(stands)
Wait -- That's Juliet's line.

FINN
(pulls her back)
SHH... we're winging it here.

LUCY
(to JAKE)
But I'm ...the NURSE. In the play. I wanted to tell you -—

NURSE
(hospital gown as nun's habit, or head scarf)
Anon, anon— lots more anons. Marry, I am the nurse, dear Juliet.

DOCTOR
What the heck?

NURSE
(worried)
Just -— go -— We're not going to dance in your precious ER. Go write your notes or something. Please?

DOCTOR
(to NURSE)
"Do you bite your thumb at me, sir?" (proudly) I was in Romeo and Juliet in college. I was Abraham.

LUCY
You were?

JAKE
Shall I hear more? Juliet?

LUCY
(smiles, gets into character, looks at JAKE)
"What man art thou that dost" something something
"stumblest on my counsel?"

JAKE
Sorry. I got nothin. Guts-gripping mangled joithead! Uh—

RA
(prompting)
"By a name, I know not—"

JAKE
That's it! "By a name, I know not how to…"

RA
"tell thee—who I am."

(LUCY remembers and jumps in.)

LUCY
"My ears have not yet drunk a hundred words…" um…

RA
(prompting)
"Yet I know the sounds."

LUCY
"Art thou not Romeo and a Montague?"

(JAKE nods vigorously. Has no clue what line's
next.)

FINN
(jumps up happily)
Forsooth—he's totally your Romeo if you be his Juliet.

(LUCY laughs)

                    RA
Who are you supposed to be?

                    FINN
I don't know. Romeo's friend?

                    JAKE
100%.

                    RA
Mercutio?

                    FINN
Sure.
          (Hoists ski pole as sword—looks at RA)
Come at me Tybalt!

                  NURSE
              (pushing RA aside)
I come anon!

                   LUCY
The nurse isn't in this scene.

                  NURSE
I've seen this play. Nobody's gonna mess with our Mercutio.

          (She grabs the other ski pole / sword.)

But I've always wanted to sword fight. En garde,
Mercurochrome!

                  (Sword fight –NURSE and FINN are kicking it
                  during the following.)

                              RA

"A hit! A palpable hit!"

                           DOCTOR

That's from Hamlet!

                              RA

Who cares?

                            LUCY

I think one of you says, "Put up your swords. You know not
what you do."

                            JAKE

Ha--That's for sure.

                            FINN

Wow. That was kind of empowering.

                           NURSE

And exhausting.
                     (sheaths her sword)
I'm out of breath.

                            LUCY

Hey, that's actually one of my –our—lines! The "out of
breath" part.

                              RA
                          (to Doc)
How do you know that line's from Hamlet?

                           DOCTOR

I was Rozencrantz.

NURSE

Well, well, alas and anon--So it's DOCTOR Shakespeare
now, huh?

DOCTOR

Drama club. A great way to meet smart women—who don't
discuss appendectomies or tracheotomies on a date.

JAKE

Did someone mention smart women—and dates?
(turns to LUCY)
Juliet—you doth make the stars shine bright.
(Reaches for her hand.)

LUCY
(smiles)
Good Pilgrim, you do touch my hand—like this.
(palm to palm)

JAKE

I… think… hope… we kiss soon…

LUCY

I'd be OK with that.

NURSE

Anon, anon—alas the day and marry!

RA
(jumps up)
You need Friar Lawrence for that!

JAKE

Whoa—marriage? Can we take it a little slower?

                              LUCY
Yes, please.

                             NURSE
And NO poison! Nobody dies on my watch.

                    (LUCY whispers to RA, who stands before
                    them, all seriousness.)

                               RA
I, Friar Lawrence, doth agree. "He stumbles that runs fast."
Therefore, Romeo—do thou give Juliet your digits anon.

                             JAKE
I think we were actually at the kissing part.

                               RA
Digits, kind sir.

                    (RA's turn at another poor pantomime of typing
                    on a phone)

                             NURSE
Anon!

                              LUCY
"If thy bent of love be honorable…"

                             JAKE
Uh…

                    (RA tries again -- pantomime of typing on a
                    phone. NURSE pulls out her actual phone to
                    demonstrate.)

LUCY

Ay me.

> (Takes JAKE's phone; types in her number, one-handed btw.)

"I gave thee mine, before thou didst request it."

JAKE

Ohhhh. *Those* digits.

> (grins; holds out his hand for her phone; she gives it to him.)

NURSE
(on her phone)
Hey—the whole play's on here! And I have more lines.
> (She points to FINN's head and reads.)
"I saw the wound. I--"

LUCY AND NURSE
(together/ But LUCY says it to JAKE.)

"Saw it with mine eyes."

> (Ambulance siren gets louder/ closer.)

DOCTOR
That's my cue, folks. Time for you to take this show on the road. And Nurse—

NURSE
I know -— not in your ER -—

DOCTOR
Thanks... actually... I needed that.

(to all)

Keep shining everyone.

(He exits)

NURSE

(A beat to process the DOCTOR's words. Then reading her phone to the rest of them)

"Go forth! Seek happy nights to happy days!"

(a chorus of farewells. JAKE takes LUCY's hand, but she looks at the NURSE. He gets it and exits.)

LUCY

(The last to leave. Hugs NURSE.)

See you at the play?

NURSE

You bet! Break a CHAIR leg, kiddo!

(LUCY exits. NURSE hoists the ski-pole / sword and fences her way off stage.)

(CURTAIN)

Yes, And…

Scene 1

> At rise, empty high school theater. Early
> January, after school. A tarp is bunched up on
> the stage floor with a few costume pieces on top.
> MIRANDA enters from main door as MRS.
> JAMES/ aka SIRI enters from the Green Room.

MIRANDA

Hey! Hi Mrs. K. Have you missed me?

SIRI

> (Upset but good at hiding it from her students.)
Hi Miranda. How's college?

MIRANDA

I love it. Well, most of it. Wait. You're not Mrs. K.

> (Double checks to make sure.)

Ha! Good one, Mrs. James. You had me there for a second,
seeing you here in the theater.

SIRI

They let me out of my room once in a while.

MIRANDA

Oooh. Have you ever pulled the twin-switch at school and
taught each other's classes?

SIRI

I'll never tell.

MIRANDA

I was just coming to say hi. I go back to school this
weekend.

SIRI

Well, she's not in the Green Room.

MIRANDA

There's no way she's left school yet.

SIRI

Very true. She's always the last one out of here.

MIRANDA

Maybe she's in storage putting costumes away.

SIRI

I wouldn't be surprised. If you see her, tell her I need to talk
to her, OK?

MIRANDA

Sure. Good to see you, Mrs. James.

(MRS. JAMES/SIRI exits and MIRANDA picks
up the costumes. Only the tarp remains. Calls
out.)

Mrs. K? You missed a few costumes! You know the students
are going to pull them all out again tomorrow! Haha. Mrs.
K?

(MIRANDA exits to storage with costumes just
as BEATRICE enters from the side door. They
do not see each other.)

BEATRICE

Wow, it feels good to be back here. Anyone home?
Wherefore art thou, Mrs. K? It's your favorite graduate
Beatrice. (beat) You have to be here somewhere. The side
door was o-- (laughs) Don't tell me you left and forgot to
lock up. Oooh–admin's gonna be on your case. Again.
Especially if they catch me here, breaking the no-students-
in-the-theater-without-a-teacher rule.

Anybody here?

        (BEATRICE squints at the back of the
        auditorium.)

Are you in the light booth? Wait–the Green Room. That's it.

        (BEATRICE exits to the Green Room as
        MIRANDA enters from storage, without the
        costumes.)

MIRANDA

Hello? I'd swear I just heard someone. Mrs. K?

        (Breathes deep, taking in all the memories.)

I guess it's just you and me, dear theater.
It feels weird to see you too. And not weird at all. Which is
— weirder.

Actually, since I'm talking to you – which is also extremely
weird – I owe you a thank you, theater. Seriously.

MIRANDA (CONTINUED)

You got me into college. That one last personal essay that was complete B.S. 500 worthless words and so many drafts about "Where do you call home?" Once I figured out it was these scratched up wooden floors, you know, it just wrote itself.

And I meant it:

'The stark, black walls of my high school theater department feel more like home than home. Theater is family when the real ones bail. Theater is where outcasts and oddballs and the occasional diva fit in, or at least coexist, most of the time...'

INTERCOM / ADMIN (OFFSTAGE VOICE OR RECORDED)

Mrs. K, please report to the office. Mrs. K, to the office please.

MIRANDA

Anyway, thanks, theater.(beat) I know, I know. You got me into my dream university and then I dumped you for Biological Science. Unfaithful wench as I am. "Pick a career that will pay the bills." So, yeah. Nothing personal. If it makes you feel any better, biology is boring compared to this.

(MIRANDA turns to exit via the stage door at the same time BEATRICE returns from the Green Room.)

MIRANDA & BEATRICE

You!

96

BEATRICE
(Surprised but happy.)
Miranda. Hi!

MIRANDA
(Icy cold in her reply.)
Well, if it isn't my long-lost EX Best Friend. Hello Beatrice.
I was just leaving. I'm sure you wouldn't want to talk to me
anyway.

(MIRANDA exits via the stage door.)

BEATRICE
That's not true! I *do* want to talk to you. Please–.

(Stage door slams. Sits on the edge of the stage.)

Great work, Beatrice. Your best friend from forever hates
you.

(Looks around. Sees audience.)

Huh. Last show I was sitting right here.
(Blinks)
I can still see the audience.

(Breaks the 4th wall. Speaks to the audience.)

How's it going? I never thought about it before, but the
audience is so important. I mean it's great when you laugh or
applaud, or cry. But you give the actors so much more than
that. You helped me realize I could do hard things. Class
presentations were a breeze after facing all of you.

BEATRICE (CONTINUED)
Even raising my hand was easier. Remember last year when
you were sitting there? And I was in my Launce costume?
My last high school play? (Beat) This was my favorite part.

(Gets into character as Launce, *Two Gentlemen
of Verona*)

**I think Crab, my dog, be the sourest-natured
dog that lives: my mother weeping, my father
wailing, my sister crying, our maid howling, our cat
wringing her hands, and all our house in a great
perplexity, yet did not this cruel-hearted cur shed
one tear: he is a stone, a very pebble stone, and
has no more pity in him than... a dog.**

(BEATRICE takes off her shoes.)

Nay, I'll show you the manner of it.

(BEATRICE smells one of her shoes.)

ADMIN (OFFSTAGE VOICE)
For Heaven's sake, Iris, stop. Hear me out. You're the only
one who can talk some sense into them.

MRS. K (OFFSTAGE VOICE)
But not all of them are my theater kids.

ADMIN (OFFSTAGE VOICE)
As your principal...

MRS. K (OFFSTAGE VOICE)
Oh wow. You're going to play that card?

ADMIN (OFFSTAGE VOICE)
And your friend.

BEATRICE
Crap.

> (Voices get closer. BEATRICE searches for a
> place to hide.)

ADMIN (OFFSTAGE VOICE)
It's not up to me. You know that.

> (BEATRICE knows she'd get caught for sure if
> she ran up the center aisle to the main theater
> doors at the back of the auditorium. She panics.
> Quickly puts one shoe on.)

MRS. K (OFFSTAGE VOICE)
I know. (sigh)

> (BEATRICE crawls to the tarp on the floor and
> hides under it. She motions for the audience not
> to give away her hiding place, as MRS. K and
> ADMIN enter. BEATRICE's second shoe, lost in
> the scramble, remains visible on stage.)

MRS. K
But we are *educators*. Our job is to give our students the
resources and confidence to form their own opinions. What
— and then suddenly we take their choices away?

> (MRS. K and ADMIN never see Beatrice under
> the tarp. Find moments or pauses in their
> conversation where BEATRICE can very slowly,
> surreptitiously crawl upstage towards the exit.)

ADMIN

You know we're on the same team. But kids exploding at this board meeting is not going to help. Talk about a tempest in a teapot.

MRS. K

Listen to you, getting literary.

ADMIN

Please talk to your students. Or else.

(BEATRICE under the tarp, reacts to the "or else" but no one sees this.)

MRS.K

Or else what?

ADMIN

They may give me no other choice but to shut it down completely.

(ADMIN steps over tarp and exits. BEATRICE sits up, about to come clean to her teacher when MRS. K speaks. BEATRICE hides again.)

MRS.K

You can't do that!

(Answers her phone.)

Hi, honey. (beat) Yeah, just another day in paradise. (beat) I'm OK. (beat) You're right. I'm not OK. (beat) Don't I wish. (beat) Ha! (beat) Except you didn't just have a lovely conversation with a certain admin. (beat) You know I can't say that! (beat) Supposedly I'm the only one who can talk

some "sense" into the kids about the school board meeting.
(beat) That's what *I* said! (beat) OK. (beat) Yes. (beat) I am
breathing! I'm just so frustrated. Between you and me, I feel
like handing in my resignation. Today.

> (BEATRICE wants to respond to this but it's no
> time to admit she's been eavesdropping. MRS. K
> doesn't see her slip out from under the tarp and
> run for the side exit. After BEATRICE's exit.
> MRS. K sighs.)

You know me too well. (beat) I could never just drop
everything and leave the kids. (beat) You're right. (beat)
Yeah, well, don't let that go to your head. (laughs) Anyway,
the school board meeting has been postponed until Monday
because of the weather. Small miracles. I'll be home soon.

> (Goes to pick up tarp.)

Yes, please. Takeout sounds perfect. Maybe we'll get lucky
and have a snow day tomorrow.

> (Hangs up. Sees BEATRICE's shoe. Picks it up.
> Looks around suspiciously. Blackout)

Scene 2

> MIRANDA sits at a small table in a small-town coffee shop, waving a menu around for emphasis as she vents to the server, HELEN, aka BEATRICE and MIRANDA's other best friend.

MIRANDA

You should have seen her: "Miranda. Hi!" Acting like nothing had ever happened! What was I supposed to say: "Gee, Hi Beatrice. Are you going to the Improv Party for Zoey tonight?" Oh shoot. She better NOT be going! Did Duke invite her?

HELEN

How should I know? Maybe he invited the whole Improv Club. I'm not sure who's in it this year. I bet Zoey's president now.

> (Realizes her boss is watching them. Speaks louder.)

May I take your order?

MIRANDA

Hot chocolate. Extra marshmallows.

> (HELEN raises an eyebrow.)

MIRANDA

What? I'm stressed out.

> (BEATRICE enters quickly, now wearing tap shoes.)

Oh great.

(MIRANDA hides behind her menu when
Beatrice goes to pull HELEN aside.)

BEATRICE

I need to talk to you.

HELEN

You realize I'm working, right?

(MIRANDA puts the menu down.)

MIRANDA

Are you stalking me?

BEATRICE

No!

MIRANDA

Interesting choice of footwear.

BEATRICE

I don't remember asking for your fashion approval.

HELEN

This is a friendly reminder I work here, and therefore you
will both be nice to each other.

MIRANDA

Only for you, Helen.

BEATRICE

I am not here to fight.

MIRANDA

Oh, let me guess. You're reprising your role in *Anything Goes*?

HELEN
(To BEATRICE)

Will this be To GO or could you both possibly TAKE your snippiness OUTside?

MIRANDA

I'd like to change my order to a long-overdue apology from Beatrice for jumping to conclusions again about why I didn't go to your graduation party and not stopping to learn my mom was in the hospital. And it's very hard to take you seriously right now when you're wearing those tap shoes. Hold the fries.

HELEN
(To BEATRICE)

Anne the Therapist said you were trying to sabotage your friendship so it would be easier to leave for college.

BEATRICE

Anne the — you were talking to your therapist about me? I don't have time for this now.

MIRANDA

Of course not. Silly me. You haven't had time since last June. For my texts. My voicemails.

HELEN

Will you sit down, and stop making a scene?

(Beatrice plops into a chair at MIRANDA's table.)

BEATRICE

This is serious. I just came from the high school.

MIRANDA

Where you were *also* stalking me.

BEATRICE

I wasn't. I swear. Mrs. K is going to quit her job!

MIRANDA

What? Is that why she was called to the office?

BEATRICE

Maybe.

HELEN

No way! (Louder) Would you like to hear about our specials?

MIRANDA

Mrs. K actually told you she was quitting?

BEATRICE

Not exactly.

HELEN

So that's two coffees, a "maybe" and a "not exactly?"

MIRANDA

"Not exactly." Some things never change.

BEATRICE
(To HELEN)

I came to get you to write a testimonial. Go to the school board meeting with me.

(To MIRANDA)
Could you write one too?

MIRANDA
Oh no. No,no,no. You know what would happen if I stormed
the school board meeting and defended Mrs. K to my MOM?
About something you "not exactly" heard?

BEATRICE
This is different.

MIRANDA
Have you SEEN the book-banning people camped outside
our house? Sure I'll just go make Mom's day even better.

HELEN
So that's two coffees and a testimonial for the school board
meeting, which is...

BEATRICE
Tonight. I think. Right?

MIRANDA
I hope so. There's been a truck parked outside our house for
a week with a sign that says ban GREEN EGGS AND
HAM!

HELEN
Would you like a stack of pancakes with those?

MIRANDA
Are you even listening to me?

HELEN
Just trying to do my job here.

MIRANDA

Right. Sorry. Hopefully they'll take their signs somewhere
else, after the meeting tonight. Anyway, if Mrs. K was
quitting, I feel like I would have heard something.

BEATRICE

Admin was talking about shutting the whole thing down.

HELEN

What thing? (beat) The theater?

MIRANDA

Are you sure?

BEATRICE

What else could it be?

MIRANDA

But why?

BEATRICE

I don't know. Remember last year when Max's parents
complained that theater was a distraction from his
academics? (beat) We need to get some other theater kids to
speak at the meeting too.

MIRANDA

Aren't they all going to the surprise party for — I mean.
Never mind.

BEATRICE

We can all go to the party after the meeting.

MIRANDA

Oh no, "we" can't.

BEATRICE

Will you please work on your testimonials first? This is important. Start writing.

Scene 3

Early evening. Same day. TAVEN's almost
empty living room in pre-party mode – meaning
TAVEN's mom, SIRI, removed all the
breakables and most of the furniture. DUKE, in
his pizza delivery attire, tries to hand TAVEN
three pizza boxes and a box of decorations on
top.

DUKE
(sings)
Ba dum, ba dum bump bump!

Happy delivery to you!

TAVEN
I know it's your job, but no song, please.

DUKE
Right. Here's the pizza, and the decorations. I'll be back as
soon as I can.

TAVEN
You're not going anywhere, Duke! The plan's already in
motion.

DUKE
I have to help at the restaurant. A big party booked five
tables and we're understaffed. You've got to stall her.

TAVEN

Stall her? How's this: Happy Twelfth Night, Zoey. Oh and guess what? Duke's not going to be here for a while, even though it was HIS idea for the party. Because he's an idiot. Also, he likes you.

Ohhh. Maybe I'll just BE you.

> (Takes DUKE's pizza delivery hat and puts it on, mimicking DUKE's voice. As the DUKE:)

Hi Zoey um SURPRISE! It's me, the Dukester. With your Birthday party do-over. Because I messed up at New Year's. And I read somewhere that a guy needs a BIG gesture to finally tell a girl – I mean you – how he feels. Er, how I feel.

DUKE

Dukester? I'm begging you, please. Don't screw this up for me.

> (TAVEN puts hat back on DUKE.)

TAVEN

ME???? My mom's already worried about your 'BIG gesture.' When I told her we were celebrating the Twelfth Night holiday, she said:

> (Grabs prop to represent Mom/ Mom's voice)

"As in the Feast of Fools? A time when everyone dispenses with normal conventions?? Not in my house. Find somewhere else to feast, fools."

DUKE

Ha. Good one. Except you left out the part where I brought
her free pizza with my extra super (sings) "Special Delivery
to you. Thanks for all that you do!" song and she said yes.

(DUKE tries to give boxes to TAVEN, who
blocks the exit.)

TAVEN

Only because pizza is one of her favorite food groups. Who
else is coming?

DUKE

Me, you, some of the theater kids from last year. You know –
Beatrice, Helen, and Miranda.

TAVEN

You're kidding.

DUKE

Why? Zoey always loved doing improvs with them. I saw
Helen at the diner and she said they're home from college.

TAVEN

So Miranda and Beatrice are friends again?

DUKE

When were they ever NOT friends?

TAVEN

Just before they graduated. Last year?

DUKE

Huh. I texted them all and no one said anything. I hope they
come.

TAVEN
Who else did you invite?
        (DUKE answers with a blank stare.)
What – that's it?

DUKE
Organizing a party is way out of my skill set.

TAVEN
Sort of like communication in general.

DUKE
I'll find some more people. Somewhere.

TAVEN
Terrific. Random strangers. My mom will be ecstatic. I can't
wait.

DUKE
Whatever you do, don't let Zoey leave. Please? I've gotta go.

TAVEN
Nope. You're the one who ditched her on New Year's. Not
me. You leave now and you're gonna make it worse.

DUKE
I know. I messed up again. I'm so not good at this girlfriend
stuff. Which is why I need to do something romantic.

TAVEN
How is ME keeping Zoey here going to help YOU be
romantic?

DUKE

We told her it would be an Improv Night, right? To celebrate
Twelfth Night? So play some improv games, eat some pizza.

(Hands the boxes to TAVEN. Sings.)

Happy delivery to you!

(stops)

I'll be back as soon as I can. Just don't tell her about the
surprise part until I'm here.

TAVEN

I don't like this.

DUKE

I promise I'll make it up to you.

(Finally notices the empty room.)

What happened to your house?

TAVEN

According to my mother, it's bad luck to have Christmas
decorations up on Twelfth Night.

DUKE

I meant the furniture? And the TV?

TAVEN

My family watched *Ten Things I Hate About You* and *Mean
Girls* over Winter Break and Mom's even more convinced
we're going to break all her fragile décor and throw the
furniture in the pool. Because — senior year.

DUKE

You don't have a pool.

TAVEN

I know. I assured her it was just a bunch of theater kids and she said, "Exactly." (beat) Are you at least going to help me put these decidedly-not-Christmas decorations up?

DUKE

I can't. I've got two more deliveries.

(Runs to the door and exits.)

You're the BEST Taven!

TAVEN

Yeah, I know.

Scene 4

> ZOEY stands outside her house, dressed for an
> impending snowstorm, car keys in hand, talking
> to a snowman, and eventually the universe.

> ZOEY

I can do this. It will be fun.

> (Does an about-face to go back into the house.)

No, it won't. Who am I kidding?

> (Talks to the snowman.)

All right, Yes, and… I'm a sucker for Improv Nights.

> (About-face to house.)

But it's supposed to start snowing soon. There's no way
anyone will show up.

> (Talks to the snowman.)

Stop looking at me that way.

> (To herself.)

Get it together, Zoey. You are standing out here talking to a
snowman.

> (To the snowman.)

Nothing personal.

(Looks up at the sky.)

ZOEY (CONTINUED)

This is the part where you give me a sign, Universe. Stay or go?

(To the snowman.)

I tried to tell Taven I'm a party-jinx. No really, I am. My birthday is on New Year's Eve. "Our little bonus tax write-off," my parents would say, endearingly.
Except having your little kid's birthday party on New Year's Eve *day* is like inviting people to those previews and ads they make you watch before a blockbuster movie. Everyone's out in the lobby buying popcorn. Or home planning their outfits or taking naps, in preparation for the big "drop the ball" festivities at midnight.

Except Duke said he'd be there tonight.

(Turns to go to her car and then changes her mind again.)

Except that's what he said on New Year's Eve.

(To the snowman.)

And there I was. Waiting. All night. Like all my little kid birthday parties on New Year's Eve.
Yes, and… I thought just once – this New Year's – it might be different. I mean, with Duke.

Plus back then we lived up a steep dirt road, the last to ever get plowed and yeah – it always seemed to snow that morning, even when we scheduled my party a week later. So

ZOEY (CONTINUED)

who could blame all those parents for keeping their kids
home?

And I appreciate Mom & Dad's efforts, truly, but trying to
play party games alone with your parents is excruciatingly
sad.

(ZOEY pats the book under her arm.)

Which is why I've learned to always bring a book to a party.
Especially ones in January.

(Looks at her keys. Looks at the universe.)
Anything, Universe? (beat) I'm going back inside.

(To the snowman.)

Thanks. You know. For listening.

(Sound of a beat-up old jalopy stopping
suddenly, and someone getting out. Duke enters
with a pizza box.)

DUKE

Zoey! Hi. What are you doing out here?

ZOEY

I um live here? I was definitely not just talking to this
snowman.

DUKE

Aren't you going to Taven's? You know for our impromptu
Twelfth Night celebration. With improvs?

ZOEY

It's going to snow soon.

DUKE

Neither snow nor sleet shall stop theater kids from Improv
Night.

ZOEY

Yeah, well.

DUKE

Wait. Please. Mrs. K would be very disappointed.

ZOEY

Mrs. K's coming to the party?

(DUKE laughs.)

DUKE

No, but remember that warm-up?

ZOEY

About — snow?

(Alternates back and forth, stepping from foot to
foot in an oddly mesmerizing pace, as he recites
ye olde theater warm-up)

DUKE

Whether the weather is cold

Or whether the weather is hot.

Say it with me.

(ZOEY does. Their pace gradually quickens to a
brisk march, arms swinging.)

DUKE AND ZOEY

Whether the weather is cold

Or whether the weather is hot.

We'll be together whatever the weather

Whether we like it or not.

  (They repeat a second time, and end up facing each other.)

Whether the weather is cold

Or whether the weather is hot.

                    (Pace slows as they connect on the last two
                    lines.)

We'll be together whatever the weather
Whether we like it or not.

ZOEY

Oh.

DUKE

I didn't mean... *together* together... I mean...

ZOEY

Of course, not.

                         DUKE
Unless
                    (ZOEY laughs softly.)
You should go to the party. It'll be fun.

                         ZOEY
Doesn't look like you're going.

                         DUKE
I have some deliveries first, but I'm coming later. I promise.

                         ZOEY
That's what you said on New Year's.

                         DUKE
I … Yeah, I guess I did say that. I couldn't leave them. And I
should have known the restaurant would be packed all night
on New Year's Eve? And, will you ever forgive me?

                         ZOEY
Nothing to forgive. New Year's Eve has never been a big
deal at my house.

                         DUKE
Are you kidding me? That's your birthday!

                         ZOEY
And you know that because?

                         DUKE
In 2nd grade you invited me to your birthday party and my
parents wouldn't let me go because of a stupid blizzard.

ZOEY

I don't remember that. I mean. Thanks for trying. I should go inside.

DUKE

Wait! Uh, so hey. I was hoping you would take this pizza over to Taven's. For the party. I forgot it was part of the delivery. For Taven. Since you're going? Please?
(Sings)
Ba dum, ba dum bump bump!
Happy delivery to you. Thanks for...

(DUKE hands the pizza box to ZOEY.)

ZOEY

Oh. OK. I guess.

(DUKE hugs her impulsively, pizza box and all. They have an awkward moment. She exits.)

DUKE

Thank you! Save a slice for me.

(Sound of ZOEY's car door, and then driving away.)

"Save a slice for me." Who Says That??? You idiot.

(DUKE exits to his car.)

Scene 5

> TAVEN is putting out folding chairs in the empty living room. Doorbell rings.

ZOEY

Hey Taven! Pizza Delivery!

TAVEN

Zoey?

> (TAVEN is about to exit to get the door but stops when their cell phone rings. TAVEN sees who's calling.)

Seriously, Duke?

> (Answers phone.)

Now what? Zoey's at the door saying she has pizza. (beat) OK. Ha — that was quick thinking.

> (Doorbell rings again.)

ZOEY

Taven! Open the door. It's freezing out here.

> (TAVEN runs far away from the door and shouts.)

TAVEN

I'm coming!
> (To DUKE)

I've gotta go. Zoey just got here. Do NOT blow this, Duke.

(Pockets their phone, takes a deep breath, opens
the door or exits and returns with a frozen
ZOEY carrying the pizza box.)

ZOEY

Geez. I could have died of hypothermia out there.

TAVEN

Happy Twelfth Night to you, too.

ZOEY

Duke said this is part of your order.

TAVEN

Yes, Indeed. It certainly is. That guy, Duke. He sure is
something. He should be here soon.

ZOEY

He told me he had deliveries.

(Looks around.)

What happened to your house?

TAVEN

My mother thinks we're going to have an out-of-control
rager.

(ZOEY pulls out her book.)

Oh, no you don't. I need you to help decorate.

ZOEY

I just have a few more chapters.

TAVEN

Not an option. Finish it later.

(ZOEY takes a Happy Birthday banner out of
the box.)

ZOEY

Is it someone's birthday?

(TAVEN grabs the banner and tries to hide it.)

TAVEN

Of course not. That's ridiculous. Whose birthday would it
be?

(ZOEY picks up a small box of index cards.)

ZOEY

What are these for?

TAVEN

My mother again. Since tonight is actually Twelfth Night,
she thought we could play Shakespeare charades. Those are
quotes from some of the plays.

ZOEY

This is what a high school English teacher thinks we're
gonna do at an "out-of-control" rager?

TAVEN

More like this is what a mom who teaches Shakespeare gives
you to make sure we don't let the raging begin.

                                    ZOEY
Right. Cause nothing says party like a box of Shakespeare
quotes.

                    (Reads one of the index cards.)

**Some are born great, some achieve greatness and some
have greatness thrust upon 'em.**

                                    BOTH
Wooo!

(Blackout)

Scene 6

> BEATRICE in clicky tap shoes, Helen, and a
> somewhat timid Miranda make their way to the
> board meeting door, perhaps marching through
> the audience.

BEATRICE

Hang on. I think we should talk about who's speaking first.

HELEN

You should go first. You got us into this.

BEATRICE

OK So I say: Members of the school board,

> (Clears her throat.)

We are former students of Mrs. K, and we wouldn't be who
we are today if we hadn't had her theater classes.

HELEN

I might not be alive.

BEATRICE

Oh, wow. You should say that.

HELEN

I'm… not sure I'm ready to share details about my personal
life in front of old people I don't know. Your mother
excluded. I mean theater and Mrs. K, and you two helped get
me through it but…

BEATRICE

It's OK. Just share what you wrote.

HELEN
(reads)
"Everyone is so big on Social Emotional Learning right now.
But what do you think the Performing Arts are? The arts give
kids a way to communicate what's bothering us. Theater
teaches you to listen, and support each other. Trust. Teachers
like Mrs. K focus on Social Emotional Learning every day. I
wouldn't be here today without her."

(MIRANDA and BEATRICE hug her.)

MIRANDA
We're so, so glad you are, Helen.

HELEN
You guys. Are you sure the meeting's tonight? Why is the
parking lot empty?

MIRANDA
There's a sign on the door.
(Reads)
"Meeting postponed due to weather." Perfect.

(They exit, possibly back through the audience.)

Scene 7

> TAVEN's living room. An hour later. No one
> else has arrived. TAVEN and ZOEY are playing
> charades.

> (TAVEN chooses another index card. There are
> several on the floor.)

TAVEN
This is an easy one.

ZOEY

I'm done. No more charades. It's depressing with just two
people.

> (TAVEN's mom, SIRI enters with a basket of
> Elizabethan costumes. She wears a long, flowing
> Renaissance gown, possibly with a hood.)

TAVEN

How about *three* people, with my mom dressed like a
medieval Red Riding Hood? Is that depressing enough for
you?

SIRI

Huzzah! How goeth the party, friends?

ZOEY

The ragers never cameth, dear Lady Siri.

SIRI

Aye, me. Well, when they do, I thought these Elizabethan
costumes might be fun.

(TAVEN is busy acting out the charade: "To thine own self be true.")

SIRI
(Guesses happily.)
OOOH! "To thine own self be true."

ZOEY
Excellent. Lady Siri can taketh my place.

(ZOEY gets her book and reads. SIRI jumps in.)

TAVEN
That's not fair, Mom. You wrote these.

(SIRI selects an index card and starts her charade turn.)

You're kidding me.

(SIRI acts out: To BEE or not to BEE. complete with buzzing.)

Ah Ha! I know this one. *Taming of the Shrew!* Kate says: "I am a wasp. Beware my sting!" Oh yeah...
(celebrates)

SIRI
Nope. Sorry. But good guess. Actually it's "To be or not to be..."

TAVEN
There were no BEEs in Shakespeare!

SIRI

Au contraire. (sings or recites)
"Where the bee sucks, there suck I:
In a cowslip's bell I lie;"

TAVEN

Mom – ew – stop. That's disgusting.

SIRI

Ariel sings it in *The Tempest*.

TAVEN

Please excuse my mother. She was just leaving.

ZOEY

Now I see where Taven gets it.

SIRI

My sister and I blame our parents. They were Bard-aholics.
(To ZOEY)
What are you reading?

(TAVEN pulls a quote from the Charades box
and reads it aloud.)

TAVEN

"Words, words, words." Geez. Why didn't I get that one?

ZOEY

It's good, but sad.

(SIRI takes the book from her.)

SIRI

Zoey! Stop that immediately. No sad books allowed at your Bir —

TAVEN

Burning! Mom! What's burning? Do you smell smoke? Are you reheating our pizza?

SIRI

Am I? Oh dear. I do. I AM!

TAVEN

Go check the oven. Hurry!

SIRI

Right. Yes. I will.

(SIRI exits. Pops her head back in.)

By the way, I did NOT mean to sound like I was forbidding you to read that book.

TAVEN

We know, Mom.

SIRI

I WOULD NEVER TELL ANYONE THEY COULDN'T READ A SPECIFIC BOOK, EVEN IF I DIDN'T AGREE WITH THE CONTENT.

ZOEY

Do you want me to go check the pizza?

No!

      (SIRI exits.)

TAVEN
Welcome to every day around here. She's super stressed about those people trying to get books banned from the library and her curriculum, and guess who hears about it every night at dinner?

(SIRI brings out a box of pizza.)

SIRI
And guess who can hear your lovely theater voice even in the kitchen?

TAVEN
Sorry.

ZOEY
I can see someone telling their own child they aren't old enough to read certain books. But how old is old enough for people they don't even know? Like teacher-age?

TAVEN
Not that you're old, Mom.

SIRI
Oh don't get me started. *Romeo and Juliet, Merchant of Venice, Twelfth Night…*

ZOEY
They want to ban Shakespeare?

SIRI

Sexual content and suicide. Profane language.

TAVEN

Mom.

ZOEY

Anyone who's ridden the school bus has heard worse.

SIRI

Careful, or they'll want to ban school buses next.

TAVEN

WOW. Gee–Thanks for the costumes, Mom.

> (TAVEN digs into the costumes. Tries things on as the conversation continues. Possibly drapes some around ZOEY.)

SIRI

The people who are complaining don't even have kids at our school. What do you want to bet they've never even heard of half the books they want banned,let alone read them?

TAVEN

And she's off!

SIRI

I'm serious. There's some banned books website where—

> (TAVEN interrupts, now in full Renaissance garb.)

TAVEN

Woo-Hooo! Party time! Can we get back to charades now?

ZOE

No!

SIRI

Ugh. Sorry. I told you not to get me started.

(Pulls a slice of pizza out of the box.)

"If pizza be the food of love, play on."

(SIRI exits to the kitchen.)

TAVEN

Duke should be here soon.

(TAVEN and ZOEY take turns reading the
following charade quotes aloud, which somehow
becomes a conversation about DUKE, or love,
or both.)

ZOEY

"Oh wonderful, wonderful, and most wonderful, and after
that, out of all whooping!"

TAVEN

"A rose by any other name would smell as sweet."

ZOEY

"The course of true love never did run smooth."

TAVEN

"The lady doth protest too much, methinks."

ZOEY

"Men have died from time to time,and worms have eaten
them, but not for love."

> (This should give the actor enough time to
> change from SIRI to IRIS/ MRS.. K. Doorbell
> rings. TAVEN jumps up but before they can get
> to the door, MRS. K comes in with an unopened
> bottle of wine. She wears a comfy bathrobe and
> snow boots.)

TAVEN

Aunt Iris!

ZOEY

Hi Mrs. K. Are you here for the Improv Party?

MRS. K

Hi.

> (MRS. K realizes they might be talking about
> the wine bottle.)

Oh. No. This is for my sister, who has apparently had a
harder day than I have. Just making a quick delivery. Is she ?

> (TAVEN points and IRIS/MRS. K exits to the
> kitchen.)

ZOEY

How do you tell your mom and Mrs. K apart?

TAVEN

My mom makes me do my homework.

ZOEY

Oh.

(MRS. K returns to the living room. TAVEN
reads another quote.)

TAVEN
"Now I will believe that there are unicorns!"

ZOEY

That's Shakespeare?

MRS. K

The Tempest.

(MRS. K bows with a flourish.)

What's the first rule of Improv?

(SIRI calls from the kitchen. Possibly
prerecorded, if using the same actor for both
roles.)

SIRI

Yes, and… It's 6:15. Time for you to stop teaching, Iris. Go
home.

MRS. K

Adieu!

(MRS. K exits via the front door. TAVEN finds
phone. Sends a text to DUKE. WHERE ARE
YOU?)

ZOEY

Duke isn't coming, is he?

TAVEN

Of course he is.

(Texts again. IT'S JUST ME AND ZOEY.GET HERE NOW.)

ZOEY

Ha — I'll believe it when I see it.

TAVEN

Yes, and... accept what your partner brings to the scene and go with it.

(Doorbell rings. BEATRICE, MIRANDA, and HELEN enter, dusted with snow.)

BEATRICE, MIRANDA, AND HELEN

Surprise!

TAVEN

Yes, AND--- WE. ARE. SURPRISED TO SEE YOU. LOOK, ZOEY. PEOPLE.

ZOEY

(Reads one more quote.)

"Oh brave new world that has such people in't!"

HELEN

What happened to your house?

ZOEY

Didn't you hear? We're having a rager.

MIRANDA

Are we too late?

TAVEN

For our Twelfth Night celebration? Just in time.

(Lady SIRI pops in with more pizza.)

SIRI

Greetings, friends. Do but choose your attire. "The apparel oft proclaims the man."

(Looks at BEATRICE's tap shoes.)

You always did know how to accessorize.

BEATRICE

I um lost one of my shoes, and they were the only back-up in my car. I'm taking a tap class at school.

SIRI

Oooh! Fun!

(HELEN tries on the costumes. MIRANDA too.)

HELEN

I think I wore this one to the Renaissance Faire last year. Thanks Mrs. -

SIRI

You may call me Lady Siri, this Twelfth Night eve.

BEATRICE

Sorry we're late. There was supposed to be a school board meeting, but they cancelled it.

SIRI

Aye, me. Just when I was escaping into a kinder and gentler
time…

(SIRI starts to exit.)

BEATRICE

We were all set to read our testimonials about Mrs. K.

HELEN

And convince the school board not to shut down the theater
department.

TAVEN, ZOEY, SIRI

WHAT?

MIRANDA

My dad even texted me his:
(MRANDA reads her phone.)
Dear School Board (and hi to my wonderful wife): I had a
teacher like Mrs. K once. You have no idea how much she
helped me in everyday life, and still does, so many years
later. Every interview I give, every time I present a new
proposal, every time I lead a workshop, I use what I learned
in her theater classes. Please support the Performing Arts.

SIRI

Hold on, a second. Who said they're shutting down the
theater? And my sister is quitting? She was just here. Why
didn't she tell me any of this?

MIRANDA

Beatrice overheard her talking to the principal this afternoon.

SIRI

What exactly did you hear?

BEATRICE

I heard… um… Admin wanted her to talk to the students. To calm them down, I think.

(SIRI gets on her cell phone. Begins pacing.)

SIRI

Hey, Iris. (Beat) What's this about losing your job? And Admin shutting down the theater? (Beat) Oh. Hmmmm…. Interesting. (beat) So I just spoke to a few of our alums. Yep — right after you left. They were all set to go to the school board meeting tonight to defend you.

(Pacing. Stops.)

Yes, that was very nice of them. (Beat) I'll certainly do that. Love you. All the world.

(Hangs up. Speaks to BEATRICE.)

So…, remember last year when we did that unit on media consumption and critical thinking skills?

(BEATRICE, MIRANDA, and HELEN nod.)

And we learned not to jump to conclusions? But instead to go directly to the source to discern whether or not the information was credible and verifiable?

HELEN

But the source was Mrs. K.

SIRI

And did you two actually hear it from Mrs. K?

MIRANDA
We heard it from Beatrice.

SIRI

And you didn't question my sister about this directly
because...

BEATRICE

I was hiding. Under a tarp?

(ALL double-take in unison.)

I went to say hi after school, but Mrs. K wasn't there.

MIRANDA

That's actually true.

BEATRICE

Then when Mrs. K came back, Admin was with her and I
didn't want to get her in trouble because I was in the theater
without teacher supervision. So. I. Hid.

TAVEN

Except, technically you aren't her student anymore.

BEATRICE

I realized that when I was hiding, but even an alumni just
popping up randomly from under a tarp would have been
weird.

Wait. She's not quitting? But Admin threatened to shut down
—

SIRI

The library. They were talking about the banned books issue.
Kids are planning to go to the school board and speak up
against the book banners. Admin wants Aunt Iris to calm
them down.

BEATRICE

But –

SIRI

She said to tell you thank you for your concern. And if
you're still here next week, you're welcome to join us at the
school board meeting. And if you're missing a shoe...

BEATRICE

I –

MIRANDA

Jumped to conclusions? Again?

SIRI

She also told me to remind you of one of the rules of improv:
There are no mistakes, only opportunities.

(BEATRICE nods. Looks at MIRANDA.)

I'm going to bed. All the world. And don't destroy the house.

(SIRI exits. ZOEY gets up to leave.)

ZOEY

I think I'm gonna head home. Before the roads get too
snowy.

TAVEN

You can't leave!

ZOEY

Yes, I can.

TAVEN

Yes, and... You're the queen of improv. Our club president.
You know all the good games. We finally have enough
people to play.

ZOEY

I'll text you some suggestions. I love you, and it's great to
see you all.

(ZOEY turns to go and practically body-slams
DUKE who bursts in the door.)

DUKE

Hi.

(A moment when ZOEY and DUKE connect.)

ZOEY

Bye.

DUKE

You're leaving?

(ZOEY tries to leave but a group of 5+ snow-
dusted PARTYGOERS (aka randomly pre-
selected audience members) enter wearing
Happy Birthday cone-hats. THEY block her exit.
Each has a party-blower noisemaker.)

                    ZOEY
It's been a night. Excuse me, whoever you are. Please
MOVE!

                    (PARTYGOERS stand their ground and blow
                    their noisemakers. TAVEN tries to get ZOEY to
                    stay, pulls that quote from before, and reads it to
                    the cone-hats.)

"NOW I will believe that there are unicorns…!"

                    DUKE AND PARTYGOERS
Surprise!!!!!

Ba dum, ba dum bump bump!
                    (They all sing.)
Happy Twelfth Night to you.
Happy Twelfth Night to you.
Happy Twelfth Night dear Zoey —
Happy Twelfth Night to you.

                    ZOEY
          (Gestures to PARTYGOERS.)
I'm sorry but, who are these people?

                    DUKE
This is your gift.

                    ZOEY
My gift?

                    TAVEN
You got her Magic Mike dancers?

                              DUKE
NO!!!!

                (PARTYGOERS reply with noisemakers.)

We closed the restaurant early because of the storm, and my
new friends here weren't done with their party so I talked
them into coming with me.
                         (To ZOEY)
You told me all you ever wanted for your birthday was
enough people to play party games. Remember?
This is your Birthday do-over.

Please forgive me. I tried to text you on New Year's. And
call. I – there's so much I want to say. I was afraid I'd mess
things up even more.

Turns out. I did.

                              ZOEY
Maybe not completely.

                             TAVEN
Hey, Zoey. What's that improv game where ten people link
arms and become one collective brain?

                (TAVEN brings 5 PARTYGOERS down stage
                and lines them up, with BEATRICE,
                MIRANDA, HELEN in between them, and
                ZOEY & DUKE who end up in the middle, next
                to each other. TAVEN makes them link arms.
                ZOEY & DUKE feel the chemistry.)

DUKE

Would you look at this? We have enough *people* to play a game.

ZOEY

Dr. Know-it-all?

TAVEN

That's the one. You guys are all Dr. Know-It-All. How do we play, Zoey?

ZOEY

Someone asks a question, and we – I mean Dr. Know-It-All – has to answer in complete sentences, one word per person. The person at the end of each sentence gets to be the end mark: "period" or "exclamation mark" or whatever.

TAVEN

Everyone got that?

(Note: If PARTYGOERS look confused, ZOEY repeats the instructions.)

Don't worry. You'll catch on. First question: Dr. Know-It-All. What is the meaning of life?

(Dr. Know-It-All answers in a complete sentence. If necessary, ZOEY coaches last person to say "period" or "Exclamation point.")

Ha --I say the Do-Over Birthday Girl gets to ask the next question.

ZOEY

This is the best present anyone's ever given me.

TAVEN

Your question, please?

ZOEY

Dr. Know-It-All, why are my friends so great?

> (Dr. Know-It-All answers in a complete
> sentence. Again, if necessary, ZOEY coaches
> last person to say "period" or "Exclamation
> point.")

DUKE

Can Dr. Know-It-All please tell Zoey how I feel about her?

TAVEN

> (Looks at Partygoers who blow their noisemakers.)

I'm not sure that's such a good idea. Just tell her, Duke.

> (DUKE gathers his courage, takes ZOEY's
> hand.)

DUKE

I um Zoey, you –

> (Doorbell rings, and MRS. K/IRIS enters during
> the following, in her bathrobe and snow boots,
> before anyone can let her in. She carries
> BEATRICE's missing shoe.)

HELEN

You've got this Duke. What's that line from The Scottish
Play? "Screw your courage to the sticking…" post? Or
point? Something sticky.

MRS. K

"And we'll not fail." Greetings, everyone. I hope I'm not interrupting.

        (She tugs on her ear and PARTYGOERS blow
        their noisemakers.)

I was sitting at home and –

TAVEN

She lives across the street. Mom went to bed, Aunt Iris.

MRS. K

Thanks, Taven. She texted me. I'm not here for her, actually.

BEATRICE

Mrs. K -

        (MRS. K walks down the line, looking for a
        match to the shoe in her hand.)

MRS. K

I found this shoe at school today, and I thought maybe one of you could tell me which Cinderella left it behind.

HELEN

Maybe you should ask Dr. Know-It-All.

MRS. K

Now that sounds like fun. Dr. Know-It-All, do you know anything about this shoe, and why I found it on stage today?

        (Dr. Know-It-All attempts to answer this. Again,
        if necessary, Zoey coaches last person to say
        "period" or "exclamation point.")

BEATRICE

It's mine.

MRS. K

Is that right? And how did it happen to end up on stage?

BEATRICE

I went to say hi. Miranda saw me. And -

>   (MIRANDA reacts like BEATRICE has almost
>   thrown her under the bus.)

HELEN

It was a perfectly innocent gesture from one of your former
students who loves you dearly – we all do by the way — and
has recently learned not to jump to conclusions.

MIRANDA

And in fact, is prepared to tap dance for us, as an apology for
oh, so many things. Right, Beatrice?

BEATRICE

That's funny.

MIRANDA

I'm completely serious. We all are. Right, people?

>   (MIRANDA tugs on her ear and the Partygoers
>   blow their noisemakers.)

BEATRICE

O.K.

>   (BEATRICE does a quick time step.)

I'm sorry?

MIRANDA
Hmmm… I feel like we need more. What's that monologue
– Bottom's speech from *A Midsummer Night's Dream*,
maybe? About being an -

HELEN
Be nice, Miranda.

BEATRICE
I only know the monologue from *Two Gents*.

(Starts tapping.)

Nay, I'll show you the manner of it.
Actually this is how I lost my shoe. Oh nevermind. Here is
my official apology, with apologies to the Bard.

(Taps her interpretation of the next excerpt of
the Launce monologue from The Two
Gentlemen of Verona, with a few improvised
edits. Give her time to think of these.)

**This shoe is my… <u>friend</u>: no, this left shoe is my…
<u>teacher</u>: no, no, this left shoe is… <u>me</u>: nay, that cannot be
so neither: yes, it is so, it is so, it hath the worser sole.
This shoe, with the hole in it, is my <u>heart</u>.**
We, heart, and soul, and I – are truly sorry.

(All applaud. MIRANDA laughs. BEATRICE is
still tapping.)

MIRANDA
That's actually pretty amazing.

MRS. K

I can honestly say I've never seen Launce's monologue as a
tap number. Well done.

BEATRICE

Are we good now? Can I stop, please? Anytime now.

TAVEN

(TAVEN takes the hands of BEATRICE,
MIRANDA, and MRS. K.)

Give me your hands, if we be friends
And <u>Taven</u> shall restore amends.

(EVERYONE looks at TAVEN.)

Hey, it's in my blood. Happy Twelfth Night! To new
beginnings.

DUKE
(To ZOEY.)

To telling people we care about them.

MIRANDA
(To BEATRICE)

And forgive them.

BEATRICE AND MIRANDA
(To HELEN)

And would do anything for them.

BEATRICE
(To MRS. K.)
Thank you, Mrs. K, for not quitting. Even when maybe you felt like it.

(MIRANDA links arms with HELEN and BEATRICE for a mini Dr. Know-It-All. This part can be memorized. MIRANDA starts:)

BEATRICE,MIRANDA,HELEN
Thank-you-Mrs.-K-for-believing-in-us-sometimes-way-more-than-we-believe-in-ourselves.EXCLAMATION POINT!

ZOEY
Who wants to go with me to the meeting next week?

(Noisemakers optional. Hands are raised.)

DUKE AND ZOEY
Whatever the weather…

BEATRICE
Permission for group hug?

MRS. K
Granted!

(ALL surround MRS. K in a group hug, a bit too enthusiastically.)

Oh, you guys. I can't even.

(MRS. K's eyes pop when they squeeze in tighter for a second.)

                    MRS. K (CONTINUED)
No, really.

          (She laughs. They ease up on the hug.)

Thank you. All of you. Ever since we were little, my sister
and I would say, "All the world," right Taven?
Before bedtime, or when one of us was leaving. To us, it
means I love you more than the moon and stars, more than
all the world.

All the world, my friends.

                         ALL
All the world.

          (Partygoers blow their noisemakers. And
          possibly ZOEY and DUKE say: "Exclamation
          Point!")

          CURTAIN